A Teacher's Guide to
FIGHTING INVISIBLE TIGERS

A 12-Part Course
In Lifeskills Development

Connie Schmitz with Earl Hipp

Free Spirit®
PUBLISHING

D1474559

ISBN 0-915793-08-3

Cover Design and Illustration: Mike Tuminelly
Cover Photography: Tim Dockter
Text Design: Nancy MacLean
Keyline: Mike Tuminelly

Free Spirit Publishing Inc.
400 First Avenue North, Suite 616
Minneapolis, MN 55401
(612) 338-2068

TABLE OF CONTENTS

Foreword and Acknowledgements

What you have in your hands is a set of curricular materials that will help you develop and teach a course on lifeskills development. If you've already read Earl Hipp's book, ***Fighting Invisible Tigers: A Stress Management Guide For Teens,*** many of the concepts presented here on stress and stress management will be familiar to you. If you haven't read this book, don't despair, but do purchase (in publishing we never say "borrow") a copy and read it carefully! It was written for junior and senior high school students, and it serves as the blueprint for this course.

For those of you unfamiliar with the term, we define lifeskills as an assortment of stress-reducing, life-enhancing strategies that keep people feeling emotionally and physically balanced. In a well-adjusted adult (or young person), lifeskills show up as a rather personal collection of health or lifestyle habits, attitudes, beliefs, and behaviors.

Lifeskills are rarely taught in a straightforward manner in our culture, particularly to young adults. When they are discussed in school, they're typically addressed inadvertently or in piecemeal style through courses in the "regular" curriculum. For instance, one readily finds the biological facts of stress, nutrition, body chemistry, physical growth, and development presented to students in health and science courses. In another corner of the school, communication skills may be practiced in speech class or student council. For upperclass students, personal goal-setting might be encouraged in individual career counseling sessions. After school, opportunities for physical exercise abound in multiple sports activities—although for many students, competitive school athletics have the opposite effect of a supportive lifeskill or relaxation strategy.

While all of these courses or activities may contain critical information that can relate to the development of lifeskills, it's up to the student to make the connections, and to pull it together in a meaningful fashion. Usually, the information supplied is superficial at best, and presented so indirectly that students fail to personalize the concepts. Similarly, the amount of time commonly allowed for practicing lifeskills is inadequate, so few of the behaviors suggested are actually implemented or maintained after the course concludes.

In contrast, this course uses an interdisciplinary approach. The psychobiology of stress and stress management skills form the thematic center of the course, and each of the twelve sessions pulls relevant concepts together from science, psychology, sports medicine, relaxation, and other content areas. The overall goal is to help students recognize their own stressors and habitual responses to stress, and to develop behaviors that contribute to physical and emotional "wellness." Also, students will spend a considerable amount of time practicing lifeskills during the course.

In **Part I: Background and Foundations,** we provide an overview of the course and its underlying philosophy and rationale. We'll explain in greater detail the concepts of stress and lifeskills. We'll discuss how lifeskills are typically acquired, and the reasons for teaching them in a course for young people. We'll introduce the materials and prepare you to use them by explaining:

- course goals, session topics, and activities

- a course evaluation

- who should participate in the course

- alternative formats for the course

- steps for implementing the course

In **Part II: Sessions Guides,** we present twelve complete, self-contained teacher guides for each of the sessions. Each guide contains: (a) an overview of the topic, (b) learner outcomes, (c) a timed agenda, (d) resources and materials, (e) description of activities (with specific instructions and scripts), (f) alternative suggestions, and (g) references. Each guide also contains overheads for the teacher, and all the basic materials that students need for that session, including handouts, worksheets, guidelines for projects, and inventories. Students will also need a copy of *Fighting Invisible Tigers: A Stress Management Guide For Teens* for weekly reading assignments.

Part III: Additional Teaching Materials contains several tools to guide evaluation of the course and student assessment. It also contains a short bibliography of titles not listed in the reference sections of each session guide.

We were fortunate to have two capable educators preview these materials. Our thanks go to Diane Heacox, District Gifted Education Coordinator for the Edina Public Schools in Edina, Minnesota, and Joel Anderson, pro-active counselor and advocate for the gifted in St. Louis

Park, Minnesota. The materials were piloted in several workshops for gifted teens during the summer of 1986 by Judy Galbraith and Earl Hipp, and with Edina school students in the fall of 1986 by Ms. Heacox.

For those of you who choose to teach the course, congratulations! You'll be accomplishing something for young people not often attempted in a school setting—or any setting, for that matter. We wish you well. We'd also like to hear how the course went—what worked well for you and what didn't. There is a short author's evaluation form in the back of this book with space for you to comment on your experiences implementing the course. Whether you teach all or just some of the sessions, please feel free to write to us in care of our publisher, Judy Galbraith, (Free Spirit Publishing Inc., 400 First Avenue North, Suite 616, Minneapolis, MN 55401) and let us know how we can improve these materials.

Connie C. Schmitz
Earl Hipp

PART I

BACKGROUND AND FOUNDATIONS

Philosophy and Rationale

As a teacher, you know the feeling of stress. You can feel it in your larger classrooms, the ones brimming over with kids—all of whom need individual help. You can feel it in the constant press for time: Where can you catch a few extra moments to prepare for a class, to reflect or think creatively about a lesson? From over-anxious parents to visiting school officials to undisciplined kids, the triggers that cause stress abound in your everyday world. And if you've survived your fifth anniversary in elementary/secondary education, you've probably learned something about coping with stress—or perhaps you haven't, but would like to soon!

People who study stress patterns in adults find that those of us who survive in stressful positions typically do develop, at the very least, some short-term coping mechanisms to get us through our worst days. Coping strategies (e.g., escaping to the teacher's lounge, drinking cup after cup of coffee, avoiding people with whom we're in conflict, working longer and longer hours, taking sleeping pills) provide a measure of immediate relief, usually by distracting or disengaging us from a difficult situation. Learning to avoid, procrastinate, or escape are all human survival techniques, but too much reliance on coping can obscure the "real" problems and make substantive change more difficult. Some forms of coping, moreover, lead to very unhealthy, destructive behaviors (e.g., alcoholism).

Some adults learn to manage stress by doing more than merely cope on a day-to-day basis, They learn to identify what causes stress and their personal stress signals. They learn to monitor the amount and type of stress they feel, just as the keeper of a dam regulates the flow of water through the gates. They build up their resources for maintaining equilibrium, and by learning, over time, more skillful responses to the demands of life. These abilities can be learned. To be a good stress manager, you need to develop stress management skills; we call them lifeskills.

What are Lifeskills?

Lifeskills are an assortment of behaviors that can reduce stress and help us maintain physical and psychological health. Examples of lifeskills are found in people who set goals, manage their time, build supportive networks, and who assert themselves responsibly. They are found in people who know how to relax and take good care of their physical health. Lifeskills are tactics that build rather than drain energy; they fortify people for living, as well as heal their wounds.

The concept of lifeskills is closely tied to the concept of stress. In fact, in this book, we use lifeskills and stress management skills somewhat synonymously. In and of itself, stress is neither all bad nor all good. Certainly, it is an important part of life. Accurately stated, "stress" is a biologically-inherited response of humans to any number of potentially threatening triggers or stimuli. When stimulated by either a pouncing tiger, a verbal attack, an abstract worry, or an unconscious nightmare, we experience a shot of neurochemicals to the brain and a succession of other physical and psychological reactions, such as increased pulse rates, rapid breathing, fear, and restlessness. This supply of energy can be very positive and useful. It can also be debilitating, and greatly detract from the quality of life.

What people do with particular triggers (stressors) and their own reactions (stress patterns) differs greatly from individual to individual. To begin with, what seems stressful to you may not seem stressful to me. What my heart would do, were I poised on the threshold of an airplane's open door, is different than what an experienced sky diver's would do because of the differences in our training, experiences, and temperaments. Even when two equally trained people are faced with the same stressful event, their perceptions—and ultimate responses—may be very different.

We believe people can learn to be more skillful in managing stress-producing situations than is commonly believed. Some of us are naturally more successful at it than others. In fact, the cave dwellers who survived in primitive eras were probably those who knew best when and how to fight or flee; they knew how to respond most appropriately to stress, and therefore, lived to produce another generation. Today's successful adults are (similarly) those people who learn how to respond to stress appropriately in self-nurturing, creative, and assertive ways. Instruction in lifeskills, therefore, doesn't simply call for superior coping strategies (i.e., better "pain relievers"— although they do have their place), but for more resourceful stress-management skills.

Consider your own experience with stress. How sensitive to stress are you? How aware are you of your coping strategies? Chances are, you've probably already discovered something about your body's unique physical response to stress. Perhaps you're all too familiar with mid-morning headaches that being behind your left eye then travel with exquisite pain to the right. Perhaps you specialize in gastric ulcers, chain-smoking, teeth clenching, backaches, or irritability. Do you continue to excel in stiff necks, sleepless nights, lethargy, or compulsive eating?

If you do, and if you pay enough attention to these clues, you may learn to predict what will cause that loss of sleep, that eating binge, or that aching back. You may recognize a cycle, a pattern, and then decide to move on to the offensive by experimenting with various remedies or "programs": Weight Watchers, aerobics, Al-Anon, jogging, group therapy, Outward Bound, Nautilus. If you find something that "works" for you—and it may be routine physical activity, more sleep, less alcohol, a better diet, meditation, daily talks with a friend, less work, more stimulating work, a different work pattern, some combination of the above, or some activity or routine altogether different—you may find yourself swearing by that method(s) because it keeps you going and makes life better.

If we chart a person's development of lifeskills in levels or stages in the fashion of Bloom's taxonomy of cognitive or affective objectives,[1] we'd probably find a staircase like the one pictured in Figure 1 (see page 10). On this staircase, one sees levels of increased awareness of stress, and increased skill in stress management.

At the lowest level of the stair we find "undifferentiated awareness of stress." When people are at the very lowest level of understanding themselves— in understanding what makes them "feel good," what makes them "feel bad," how they react to challenging or unpleasant stimuli, and what they can do to keep themselves in the comfort zone—they often do not realize how much emotional pain or physical discomfort they're already in. The pain messages, some of them quite intense, are undifferentiated. In an undifferentiated state, all stressors feel alike, or they aren't felt at all. Absence of feeling (as in apathy, lethargy) signals a heavy defense system of denial or suppression that is "protecting" a person from perceiving the pain.

At the next level in the taxonomy of lifeskills, "heightened awareness," stress as a sensation begins to have distinct qualities. A person at this stage can tell the difference between butterflies in the stomach before an exam and nausea from the flu. Coming home alone to an empty house incites a different kind of panic than receiving a public award. At Level 2, a person understands that stress has different intensities and durations. ("I thought about his phone call all night." "When I interview for a job it takes me at least three days to recover." "I'm still not used to Dad being gone.") Some stresses are labeled "good," others are "bad."

Persons at the next level "personal awareness" can now describe their personal pattern or cycle of stress in more detail. Sources can be named and "overloads" predicted with some accuracy. ("I know if I

Figure 1

TAXONOMY OF LIFESKILLS DEVELOPMENT

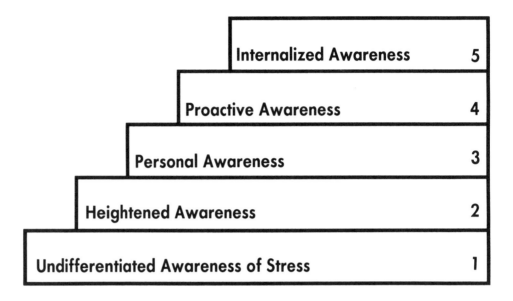

Internalized Awareness	5
Proactive Awareness	4
Personal Awareness	3
Heightened Awareness	2
Undifferentiated Awareness of Stress	1

have this third cup of coffee I'll have the biggest headache around 4:00 p.m., but I just can't stop myself.'') At this stage people have learned enough about their own bodies, minds, and habits to know what their levels of tolerance are for long work hours (for example), or "hassles," airplane noise, junk food, late-night parties, or interfering in-laws. These individuals also can identify some of the ineffective ways they've used to block stress in the past.

At the fourth level of lifeskills development "proactive awareness" individuals shift from passively reacting to stressors, to asserting some controls over them. When possible, they now choose to moderate or eliminate sources of negative stress within their environment, and to search out alternative behaviors that give back a sense of strength, energy, or peace. Although not all of the attempts made at this stage will be well thought-out, consistent, or "successful," they represent concerted effort. More consistently than before, people at Level 4 are learning to reject the "false gods"—the chemicals, the quick-fix habits, the anaesthetics, the compulsive behaviors (and we all have them, from workaholism to alcoholism)—and are less willing to be seduced by immediate relief.

The final step "internalized awareness" is to actually do for ourselves that which we know is good. People at this level are "working their routine." They have figured out what they need to do in order to stay reasonably healthy, vital, and "together." They apply this self-knowledge with enough consistency to feel and to value its benefits. And because life is never stagnant, people at this highest level continue to branch out and experiment with variations of their lifeskills as they grow older or their situations change. They think proactively of keeping their resources high; they are prepared for unknown "tigers."

How are Lifeskills Typically Learned?

As the above scenario and taxonomy indicate, it takes a long time to develop lifeskills, and it's not as easy as climbing a staircase. Most of us have to work at it and continue to refine our strategies throughout our lives. Although lifeskills are probably acquired somewhat sequentially and correlate with age and maturity, the process remains reiterative; we often cycle back to work through earlier stages in order to move forward.

Most of us do not learn lifeskills in school or by thinking about the whole matter hypothetically, however. We learn through experience. It's likely by way of traumatic experience that we learn our limits—or the limitation of our preferred coping strategies. For example, some of us learn to slow down and relax as a result of a serious accident or illness. Others learn through divorce the importance of relationships, intimacy, or assertiveness skills. We can learn from depression the benefits of "getting out," visiting friends, volunteer work, or a special hobby. Some of us can learn from a friend or relative's "bad" experience—a parent's addiction, a co-worker's anorexia. Certainly many of us learn key lifeskills by watching healthy people engage in life successfully. **But a question worth asking is, why do we learn so late?**

Why Do We Learn Lifeskills So Late?

1. No one teaches us the facts about stress.

One answer is that no one taught us anything about stress; that a certain amount of stress or stimulation is normal and good; that it's okay to pay attention to the clues your body gives you; that you can gain some control over the amount and type of stress you face. Schools aren't often able or willing to teach students the physical or psychological facts of stress. Although academic, social, and other performance expectations escalate yearly for students as they progress through the system, few teachers or parents counsel them on handling the pressure this creates *before* a crisis occurs.

2. Many "unwritten" societal norms create stress.

Second, many cultural norms in our society do not support a moderate lifestyle or pace of life. These norms say: "Be first," "Winning is everything," "Don't be lazy," "Get ahead and make something of yourself," "Don't show your pain." It's common for television ads to tell teenagers "Go to the limits," "Be wild and crazy," "Make it big," while parents and teachers are saying "Work up to your potential." Sociologists studying leisure time habits in this country find that lots of people don't really know what it means to relax. Despite unprecedented affluence, Americans "labor to find the time for leisure pursuits."[2] According to the *Wall Street Journal*, only the Japanese are considered less able to relax, more competitive during "off-hours," and more likely to superimpose business onto leisure time activities than contemporary American business men and women.

3. There are few models who manage stress well.

A third reason we learn about stress "so late" is the lack of healthy role models. Father does not typically announce at breakfast that he's nervous about a presentation and will therefore meditate in the living room; instead, he barks at mother for burning the toast. We don't usually take the time to educate ourselves about the skillful handling of stressful life events. Instead, we deny how stressed these events make us feel. We interpret stress as personal weakness, suffer in silence, or declare war on whatever (or whomever) seems responsible for our discomfort.

4. There are few role models to talk to young people about stress.

Finally, our culture doesn't really know how to encourage children and young adults to develop long-term, healthy behaviors in an honest way. We may lecture the morality of not smoking or drinking and enforce strict rules, but this is different from listening to a young person's experiences or perception of stress, then problem-solving with him or her to find better ways to manage stress. A child may hear, "You shouldn't feel that way," rather than "I understand that you've had it up to here. Would you like to talk about it?" Highly judgemental reactions to an ill-chosen coping strategy deny the reality of the young person's struggle with life and anxiety. Adults lose additional ground when we lecture kids on so-called healthy habits but fail to demonstrate those behaviors ourselves. A perfectionistic, depressed, hopeless, angry, or workaholic parent or teacher doesn't offer the troubled teenager a very hopeful picture of adulthood, or many reasons for wanting to grow up.

As a result, children learn to "live with it" the way the adults in their lives "live with it." Most of us fall into massive, unconscious adaptation to constant stress. For many people, that means accepting and adjusting to their own discomfort and loneliness. After a while, the stooped back feels okay, it only hurts to straighten it. And the "high" that was good enough yesterday is not high enough for today.

Summary

In summary, inappropriate response to stress accounts for mental and physical illness among adults and children. It leads to a stunted life, one without much joy. Many of these inappropriate behaviors begin in childhood, only to come full bloom in adolescence or adulthood What teenagers don't know about stress, and their own resources for moderating stress, can be very "serious business."

For example, nine percent of all adolescents in Minnesota are estimated to have severe clinical depression.[3] Three of the 10 leading stressors of adolescents are school-based, and one in every ten suicides is related to a crisis at school. The national suicide rate among teenage girls has more than doubled in the last two decades; for teenage boys it has tripled. Suicide is now the second leading cause of death among 15- to 19-year-olds. Two million American kids attempt suicide every year. This means that every 90 seconds a suicide attempt occurs; every 90 minutes a suicide attempt is "successful." The suicide rate of teenage boys in the United States "now surpasses those of all other nations in the world—including Japan and Sweden, long identified with a suicide problem".[4]

What this adds up to is a rationale for teaching students a set of lifeskills. Many of us learn "too late" about stress by experiencing its powerfully negative side effects. Unquestionably, some students will profit by the mistakes of others and the examples of healthy role models, but the learning of lifeskills should not be left to unconscious modeling, or to trial and error. It does not take time and maturity to shape healthy behaviors, but this process should, logically, be accompanied with direct instruction, discussion, and support.

Course Description

Course Goals

The overall purpose or aim of the course is to raise students' awareness of lifeskills. This means beginning with students at whatever level of awareness they're at (Completely denying stresses? Beginning to differentiate between stressors? Understanding the difference between coping and management? Ready to try some new strategies?) and bringing them up to a higher level. This should be considered an introductory level course; students are not expected, therefore, to progress from the lowest level of awareness of lifeskills to the highest after only twelve sessions. Although the benefits of relaxation or communication skills are great, and tempt us to state lofty goals and promise terrific results, realistically we know it takes a long time to refine and incorporate these skills into our everyday lives.

This overall aim translates into seven specific goals. Each goal reflects a particular level of lifeskills development on the taxonomy. All levels are represented except for the highest, Level 5, attainment of which would be difficult to measure in a short-term period. (How do you know whether students have internalized long-term habits after observing them for only 12 sessions?) And while we hope that some students will make strong, enduring commitments to new lifeskills, we don't expect many kids to progress to this level on the first try.

Learner Outcomes

The goals of the course are to enable students to:

1. Differentiate between a state of stress and a state of relaxation (Level 1)

2. Understand the origins and nature of stress (Level 2)

3. Describe their physical and emotional responses to stress (Level 3)

4. Evaluate their current stress levels and their current methods for coping (Level 4)

5. Recognize the difference between positive and negative coping and proactive stress management (Level 4)

6. Identify the benefits of a range of lifeskills: physical activity, relaxation, assertiveness, supportive relationships, and life planning (Level 4)

7. Practice new skills for stress management (Level 4)

These seven goals provided the framework around which the course content was developed. They also form the basis for student and course evaluation. In addition to these goals, learner outcomes have been identified. These are listed at the beginning of each session guide.

Course Content

In selecting content for the course, we concentrate on five of the six lifeskill areas discussed in *Fighting Invisible Tigers: A Stress Management Guide For Teens* These areas are: (1) physical activity, (2) relaxation, (3) assertiveness, (4) supportive relationships, and (5) life planning. We selected these five because they seem to have the broadest application and are not typically addressed in the school curriculum. Theoretically, however, a whole host of strategies could be called "lifeskills," because what makes a particular activity life-enhancing or stress-reducing depends on the individual who uses it.

Each of these areas has been developed into one or more fifty-minute sessions and/or woven into the fabric of suggested teaching strategies.

The sessions have been designed so that each unit focuses on a few developmental levels at a time, beginning with Level 1 on the taxonomy of lifeskills and working up to Level 5. These levels of awareness are listed below, along side of the session number and topic.

Course Sequence

Session	Topic	Level of Awareness
1.	Orientation to Lifeskills	1
2.	Life in the Jungle	1, 2
3.	Coping vs. Stress Management	1, 2, 3
4.	Getting Physical	1, 4
5.	The Eye of the Hurricane	1, 4
6.	Communication Styles	1, 4
7.	Being Assertive	1, 4
8.	Friendship Levels	1, 4
9.	Weaving a Safety Net	1, 4
10.	Scripting the Future	1, 4
11.	Planning for Change	1, 4
12.	Moving On	4, 5*

(Key to Levels of Awareness: 1 = undifferentiated awareness; 2 = heightened awareness; 3 = personal awareness; 4 = proactive awareness; 5 = internalized awareness.)

*Level 5 is listed here because the final discussion encourages students to form long-term contracts with friends or supportive adults to maintain certain lifeskills. (See Session 12.)

If you need to make the course shorter, start by deleting Session 12 and combining Sessions 1 and 2. To accomplish this in a six-week course, proceed to combine each of the double sessions (i.e., those on assertiveness, relationships, and planning) into one. You'll have to decide which of the remaining sessions seems least important; perhaps the availability of teaching staff will influence your decision here. To condense the amount of homework, double up reading assignments, possibly reduce the number of student inventories, and select only one final project for students to complete. You'll also need to make accompanying adjustments in the course evaluation questionnaire.

To extend the course to a full semester, spend more time "rehearsing" each lifeskill area. Many more exercises are available in various texts on assertiveness training, communication skills, planning, and time management. Nutrition is a topic which we excluded, but could certainly be included given a longer course format. Additionally, an emphasis on drug awareness and chemical dependency could be built into the earlier sessions on coping strategies.

Learning Activities

Most sessions begin with some presentation of content by the teacher that leads into small group exercises or discussion. Many of the learning activities engage students either in a role-play or direct experience (e.g., meditation, aerobic exercise). The learning activities suggested for the earlier sessions of the course require little or no self-disclosure; they are "low risk" for the student (and teacher!). As the course progresses and group members (presumably) become more familiar and trusting of each other, the activities start to require more interpersonal sharing. None of the activities are confrontational, however, and students should always maintain the right not to participate. Most discussions and activities are suitable for groups with between five and twenty-five students.

Course Evaluation Plan

Student Evaluation

As we mentioned earlier, this is an introductory level course that focuses on personal awareness and growth. The thrust of the evaluation should be in concert with that focus. It's more important, we believe, for students to make relatively small steps in identifying their personal stressors and response patterns than in attempting a highly sophisticated understanding of any single component.

The evaluation plan, therefore, calls for the assessment of how much personal awareness students gain as a result of the course. Although some of these gains may not show up for months and even years, students can learn a lot about themselves in twelve sessions. The evaluation plan therefore translates into the question: "Are students more aware of their stress response(s) and more proactive in maintaining emotional, physical balance after the course than before?" This question should guide all subsequent efforts to evaluate students and course effectiveness.

Progress of this type is highly individual. It can be best assessed by observing students' behavior in class, by listening carefully to their in-class contributions and by examining their final projects. To help teachers make these kinds of observations, we've developed a matrix that illustrates each developmental level of lifeskills awareness with sample behaviors. (This Lifeskills Matrix can be found in Part III, page 129). Theoretically, students' progress can be charted by the teacher (or co-teacher) quite systematically by using this behavior matrix, which is based on the taxonomy of lifeskills development. To do this, teachers take a "reading" of each student during the first few sessions, and again during the final sessions. The "reading" consists of classifying a student's comments, behavior, questions, and projects according to behaviors on the matrix.

A second way to look at students' growth is through a series of student self-inventories. Student inventories are used as homework assignments after Sessions 2, 4, 5, 6, 8, and 10. Essentially, there is one inventory for each of the five lifeskill areas, and one on general awareness of stress. The inventories cannot directly show student progress that is gained as a result of the course, but they do provide you with information on where students are in terms of lifeskills development. What's probably more important, they reveal this information to students. In this respect, the inventories are good teaching tools, as well as instruments that collect assessment data.

A third way to assess student progress is by evaluating their final projects, which are described in detail in the student handouts contained in Session Guides 4 and 5. (These are the sessions in which the final projects are assigned.) There are two final projects: a twenty-minute relaxation tape that students make for themselves, and a three-to-five page personal growth contract. Guidelines for how to evaluate the projects can be found in **Part III: Additional Teacher Materials** (see pages 131).

Student Course Evaluation

Although the course evaluation questionnaire in Part II is fairly self-explanatory, readers should be reminded that the person who benefits most from these evaluation results is *you*. Therefore, don't omit this opportunity! You will benefit first and foremost because students will tell you what "worked" and what "didn't work" about the class.

Another way to assess the effectiveness of the course is to look at the "gains" students make in their awareness, as reflected by the teacher's observations, the student inventories, and final projects. Additionally, several items on the course evaluation form ask students to comment on what they learned.

Who Should Participate in the Course?

The course was designed for adolescents in a regular school setting. Our hope is that most, if not all, the sessions will be incorporated into a quarter or semester course taught by a counselor or health, social studies, or science teacher. The materials may also be appropriate for church groups, 4-H, YMCA, or other community education agencies. Teens in chemical dependency programs, "aftercare" treatment, or other therapy or support groups also could benefit from lifeskills development. Although the materials were written with "prevention" (that is, proactive management of stress) in mind, the basic concepts and strategies certainly apply to kids who've reached a crisis and need a "cure" (that is, more effective lifeskills).

As with any interdisciplinary course, it may not be immediately clear who should or could teach this course. Does it belong in science, health, or psychology? Do all kids need it, or only those seeing a counselor after school? Does it belong in a homeroom, gifted education, or special education class? Could a concerned gym teacher with a desire to do more than sex education and drug awareness teach the course?

Depending on what type of school you have, the course can work in any of these settings, and it can be taught by any of the educators found there. It could also be team taught if one teacher is responsible for coordinating all the sessions. This main teacher is responsible for bringing in the co-teachers or "guest" faculty, for explaining the purpose and philosophy of the course, and for course and student evaluation. Guest faculty are enlisted to contribute their areas of expertise, such as group dynamics, health, meditation, or assertiveness training. Expert personnel to draw upon include the school nurse, psychologist, science teacher, college counselor, and physical education teacher.

More important than any particular content expertise, is the teacher's overall interest in stress management, and his or her interpersonal style with students. The main teacher should have good group process (facilitator) skills and feel comfortable with a degree of personal disclosure. She or he should be able to set the tone for class and be an appropriate role model (e.g., accept diversity of behaviors and opinions, be willing to learn a new skill such as meditation). Not a lot of specialized knowledge is necessary; the intellectual concepts of stress and relaxation are not difficult to grasp. Successful teaching of the concepts does require that teachers value the skills and believe in their importance to teens.

GENERAL CAUSES OF STRESS

parents expecting me to be perfect

parents expecting me to have perfect friends

the pressure to do drugs

being made fun of by other kids

the pressure of grades

the loss of a friend

parents who fight

parents who constantly expect me to outdo previous achievements

having a depressed friend

having too much to do

teachers expecting too much

getting in fights with people

feeling like I have to compete, do better than my friends

lack of common interests with others

people saying ''dumb'' (hurtful) things

not being able to talk (communicate) with other people

kids getting angry at me for knowing the answers

brothers and sisters getting on my nerves

teachers who embarrass me

19

When teaching any course for the first time, it's helpful to begin with an idea of how knowledgeable or skillful your students already are in the content area you're discussing. For this reason we asked ourselves:

■ How aware of stress (on the average) are students?

■ Can they describe it, name sources, differentiate between "good" and "bad" stressors, between a manageable and intolerable amount of stress?

■ How advanced are their lifeskills? Can they identify and apply various life-enhancing or support strategies? Are they learning from the strategies that backfired? Are they exercising some control over the amount or type of stress they face?

You'll want to get a feel for this when you begin working with your students. Chances are, they'll be somewhat aware of different stressors, but only beginning to identify personal stress patterns. They may be able to say "Life is tough," or "I feel weirded out," even "stressed out." In one workshop session, gifted teenagers were able to list sources of stress and stressful situations related to school (see page 19). But few students have enough personal insight to understand the ways in which they contribute to these habitual stress reactions and patterns. For the most part, they (like many adults) blame others for their misery rather than take responsibility for their situation. They are unconsciously adopting the coping mechanisms sanctioned by their peer group (or those exhibited/enforced by parents). In terms of our taxonomy of lifeskills, this puts the majority of kids at the middle to low end of the scale.

Steps for Implementing the Course

Before teaching the course we recommend the following preparation:

1. Read *Fighting Invisible Tigers: A Stress Management Guide For Teens.*

2. Review additional readings on relaxation, meditation, physical exercise, and communication skills, particularly if you are not already teaching these subjects or aren't fairly well-versed in them. This book does not supply you with "scripts" of *every* discussion you need to lead on these topics, and you should feel comfortable elaborating on the major concepts. References are supplied in each session guide, and a short bibliography is in Part III. But don't hesitate to check out the school library or tap your own private collection.

3. Line up your support team. Talk about the materials, discuss the suitability of the suggested activities, and plan your time. Find one group of students (one class or special grouping) on which to pilot the materials, and assess their level of lifeskills awareness using the matrix in Part III.

4. Practice the relaxation exercises ahead of time. By rehearsing with people you'll learn how to modulate your voice, time your cues, and respond to the crowd's "jittery flutters" or whispering. Any group new to relaxation will invariably have some students who find this activity scary or embarrassing. Be prepared for this and a wide assortment of other reactions as well, such as yawning, falling asleep, and uncontrolled giggling. Practice will help you to sustain the mood and continue on in a relaxed manner. Similarly, if you're unfamiliar with aerobics, practice the exercise suggested in Session 4 ahead of time with friends, students, or other teachers. This will help prepare you for the range of physical abilities you'll likely find in the class.

References

[1]Bloom, B. S. (Ed.). *A Taxonomy of Educational Objectives: Handbook I, the Cognitive Domain.* New York: Longmans, Green and Co., 1956.

[2]"Working at Relaxation." Special Report: The Business of Leisure, *Wall Street Journal.* Monday, 21 April, 1986, p. 1.

[3]Minnesota State Board of Education. "Resolution on Teen Suicide: An Issue for the State Board of Education and the Minnesota Department of Education." Position Paper adopted June 10, 1986.

[4]Hafen, B. and Frandsen, K. *Youth Suicide, Depression and Loneliness.* Evergreen (Col.): Cordillera Press, Inc., 1986.

PART II

SESSION GUIDES

Session 1

ORIENTATION TO LIFESKILLS

Overview

Lifeskills are an assortment of life-enhancing, stress-reducing behaviors that can be learned in order to maintain physical and psychological balance. These skills are not frequently taught in one course or setting. Rather, most people learn them through life experience, by trial and error, and by putting bits and pieces of knowledge together from different sources. In this session, lifeskills are defined and a twelve-part course is outlined. The initial distinction between stress and relaxation is experienced in a progressive relaxation exercise.

Learner Outcomes

The purpose of this session is to help students to:

1. Prepare for the course

2. Identify a range of lifeskill areas

3. Identify some of the cultural norms surrounding lifeskills (or affective) education

4. Compare the feelings of deep relaxation with those of stress

Agenda

In order to accomplish these outcomes, teachers need to:

1. Orient students to the course (5 min.)

2. Describe lifeskills, why we need them, the prerequisites for learning them (15 min.)

3. Lead a group discussion on the cultural norms surrounding affective education (15 min.)

4. Conduct a progressive relaxation exercise (15 min.)

5. Assign homework for next session

Resources and Materials

- Student Syllabus (see pages 34-35)

- The Lifeskills Circle (see page 33)

- Carpeted classroom or floor mats (optional)

- Overhead projector (optional)

Activities

1. Orientation

After handing out the syllabus, "walk through" the goals of the course. You may elaborate upon these or rephrase them in your own words, but make sure you get across the dual emphasis which is to: (1) raise students' level of awareness to their own personal stress levels and methods of coping (both positive and negative), and (2) increase their range of skills for managing stress.

Continue on through the course syllabus so that students have a general idea of the topics you'll be covering. Indicate that a variety of activities will occur; group discussions, relaxation exercises, communication and other skill-building activities.

Tell students that there are two final projects due at the end of the course in addition to weekly assignments. The assignments consist of readings (listed on the syllabus) and six self-inventories. The final projects are: (1) a relaxation audio tape that students script and record for themselves, and (2) a three-to-five page personal growth contract. The growth contract will be in an area of their own choosing and nonacademic in nature. What occurs in class will prepare them for these projects. Indicate that they won't need to begin final products until the middle of the course, and they'll have opportunities to consult with you during class time.

2. Describe lifeskills

Review for yourself the foreword and **Part I: Background and Foundations** of this book. When defining lifeskills for students, explain that they theoretically include any behavior that:

- reduces stress over the long-term

- gives a person more control over stress-creating experiences

- "gives back" strength, energy, peace; enhances life

- promotes a sense of wholeness, of healthy psychological and physiological balance.

Give some examples of lifeskills, then explain that in this course you'll be concentrating on just five major skill areas: physical activity, relaxation, assertiveness, supportive relationships, and life planning skills. Outline these areas by presenting the Lifeskills Circle (use as an overhead or student handout). Explain that the "empty" pie slice in the circle indicates that other lifeskill categories are possible, such as spirituality, creative pursuits, hobbies, and special interests. Students should feel free to consider what other lifeskill areas are important for them. Ask if anyone can provide an example of another lifeskill area, perhaps one that they currently rely on.

The Lifeskills Circle also indicates different levels of awareness in each skill, ranging from one (low) to five (high). (These levels correspond to the taxonomy of lifeskills, but the connection doesn't have to be explained here.) Students will be estimating their levels of awareness several times during the course as new skill areas are introduced. By the twelfth session, they'll be able to assess their current level of development on the Lifeskills Circle. This will give them an idea of how in (or out) of balance their skills are. In this way, the Lifeskills Circle creates a visual symbol of development in stress management ability.

In order to learn stress management skills, people need to have four things: a supportive environment, some structured learning, practice, and self-acceptance. You're there to provide the supportive environment and structured learning. You want to encourage students to be patient with themselves, and accept where they are with stress and lifeskills. Explain that it does take time to change one's life style habits. Some of the skills applied here in class may feel awkward at first, but with time and patience their benefits will become impressively clear.

3. Lead discussion on group norms

Eliciting students' understanding of societal norms is one of the themes that runs across the sessions. In this first session, ask students what they think the purpose of school is. Their answers are bound to reflect an orientation to cognitive achievement: "To make us learn . . .

math, English, and stuff . . . " "To get us a job . . . " "To get us into college." Comment on how affective education may seem different from these traditional goals.

Ask whether anyone can define affective education. Affective education concerns self-knowledge, personal growth, and understanding one's values, beliefs, and feelings. Knowledge in these areas is vital to growing up. Lifeskills are practical skills that rely on self-knowledge. They are extremely important, yet they're rarely taught in schools or discussed in families. As a matter of fact, our society often seems to act as though "feeling" issues — such as stress, need for relief, coping, finding ways to survive — don't exist. Most of us, as a result, try to deal with the pressure individually, when in fact, we need the advice and support of others.

Tell students that this class may seem different and therefore a bit uncomfortable at times. Nothing you'll be doing is intended to be "scary," but it may feel awkward and at times difficult. Some of it is going to be new for you, as well, but you're excited about the opportunity to learn with them.

4. Conduct progressive relaxation exercise

Lead into this exercise by explaining to students that often we're unaware of the load of stress we're carrying around. We get so used to this load it actually feels "normal" . . . normal to be constantly fatigued, or hyper, or sick. We accept and accustom ourselves to a high undercurrent of tension. It then takes something really unusual (CLAP!!) to wake us up.

The word CLAP above is your signal to actually clap your hands as loudly and dramatically as possible. If you aren't good at clapping, slap a ruler hard on the desk, slam a door or desktop, or shout "HEY!" at the top of your lungs. The point is to induce the fight or flight response in students — to startle them unexpectedly. This can be done quite effectively by walking in between the rows of desks, or turning and facing students suddenly.

Before the students recover from the "shock," ask them to describe the physical sensations they just experienced. Get them to verbalize the symptoms such as "stomach dropped," "eyes blinked," "held my breath," and write these on the board. Tell them that these reactions are part of the fight or flight response; this response will be the subject of several upcoming sessions and is important for understanding stress. Today, you want them to compare the sensations they just felt with a feeling of deep relaxation.

If possible, have students lie down on the floor for this exercise. If there are no mats and the room is uncarpeted, students should separate their chairs and relax as best they can in their seats. You will need to modify the relaxation script if this is the case. The exercise takes about twelve minutes.

When conducting the progressive relaxation exercise, remember to keep your speaking rhythm very slow, and pause for several long seconds after commas and periods. The best way to perfect this timing is to rehearse with someone who actually practices the relaxation exercise as you speak. The pauses should get even longer towards the middle of the exercise, when the students are at their most relaxed point. When it's time to bring the students back, quicken your speaking pace. Make your voice stronger and louder, as though to reinforce the message that it's time to return.

The script can be literally read but the exact words don't need to be memorized. It's more important that you understand the flow of the exercise. The exercise may be more effective if you tailor the script or put it in your own words. Essentially, you're inviting students to relax each part of their bodies one step at a time. To do this, you begin at the feet and move upwards, and have them visualize particular muscle groups or body sections one at a time, then together. We've highlighted the more common areas of the body that hold tension, but you may substitute others (your own!) or invite students to concentrate specifically on any "trouble spots" that resist letting go.

When reading this script, it may sound repetitious. When you are relaxing, giving in to the experience of "letting go," this repetition is necessary and comforting. Don't be afraid to repeat things several times; also don't be afraid to let silence prevail. And finally, don't underestimate the value of suggesting to students that they end the exercise with a smile. Encourage this by smiling yourself, and looking directly at them.

Progressive Relaxation Script

Lie on your back with your eyes closed, your hands at your sides with the palms facing up. Begin to let go of all the control you exert over your body; allow the feeling of relaxation to take over. Slow down your breathing, make it rhythmic. If you can, keep your mouth closed and feel the breath pull in and release through your nose only. As the breath fills your lungs, your abdomen should rise.

You're going to progressively relax each part of your entire body. Take a long, deep breath, then slowly release it. As you let the breath out, let go of all the tension in you. Allow your whole body to relax. Now, begin thinking specifically of your feet. Send a visual message to your feet. Tell them to release any feeling of tightness. Make them loose and soft. Next, release any tension in your calf muscles and around your knees. They feel calm. Now visualize the muscles in the thighs getting softer, letting go. Tell your legs to relax, to be still.

Keep breathing as you send a message to your hips and buttocks to release. Let the tension out; let them relax. Allow the feeling of relaxation to spread throughout your stomach and back like a warm glow. With each breath you feel calmer and stronger. Your stomach and back and legs and feet all feel very heavy, very relaxed. Concentrate now on your chest and shoulders. Let your lungs increase fully, now let them release fully. Let all the tightness in your chest go. Let your shoulder blades sink into the floor. Let gravity pull your spine and shoulders down towards the floor. Let all your upper body relax.

Feel all the tension slide past your shoulders and down your arms. Your arm muscles are relaxing and getting soft. Let all the tightness go. Relax your forearms, wrists, your hands. The tension is flooding out through your fingertips. Stop holding them up and in, let them relax.

Now visualize the muscles that support your neck and head all day long. Tell them it's time to rest. Let the floor support you, it's time to relax. Release all the tightness in your throat. Allow the muscles in your chin, your cheeks, and your forehead to relax. Your face feels good. Feel the tension lift from your eyes, let the feeling of relaxation spread from your eyes, like rings of water spread around a stone. Relax. Time to rest. The muscles in your scalp are relaxing, your head feels loose and clear.

Your whole body can now relax as gravity pulls it towards the floor. Breathe in and out. Your heels, calves, thighs, shoulders, back, arms, hands, face, and head are very relaxed. Your whole body feels heavy, relaxed. Gravity will do all the work. Let your body go.

Now, with the body resting quietly, focus on your breath. Feel the soft air passing in and out, and the gentle rhythm of breath, like waves, coming in and going out. Inhale life-giving, quiet energy. Exhale worries and tension. Your body is resting quietly. Breathe slowly and deeply. Concentrate on your breathing. Nothing is more important now than your breath and the quiet, calm feeling in your mind and body. You're very relaxed, but alert.

Remember this place, remember these feelings. Create a memory to use later when you need it. Remember: this feels good. Tell yourself, this feels good. Relaxation and quiet feel good.

It's time to come back now. Remember where you've been, then decide to come forward. Nourished and ready to return, begin by assuming control of your breathing. Take a good deep breath, spread energy throughout your system. Feeling positive, charged, visualize this new energy as it moves out from your center and spread over your body. See it going down your arms into your hands — now let your fingers move.

Continue these deep energizing breaths. Take deep inhalations and strong exhalations, a bit faster than before. You need new energy. It's moving down the front of your body and into your legs—now let your feet move. Feel this energy move into your face and head. Your body is ready to move. Arrive fully in the moment. Let your eyes open. Let a smile grow on your face as you sit up. Stretch—you feel good! Let's stand up now. You're done.

5. Homework

Assign students page 1 - 25 of *Fighting Invisible Tigers*.

Alternate Suggestions

Any number of relaxation or visualization exercises could be used to introduce the sensation of stress and relaxation. There are commercial relaxation audio tapes: try your local college campus bookstore, or other vendors specializing in health or psychology materials. Refer to the list of books below or in the bibliography. Also, you may write your own scripts.

Recommended Reading

Hendricks, G. and Wills, R. *The Centering Book.* Englewood Cliffs (NJ): Prentice-Hall, Inc. 1975.

Samuels, M. and Samuels, N. *Seeing With the Mind's Eye.* New York: Random House and The Bookworks, 1975.

LIFESKILLS CIRCLE

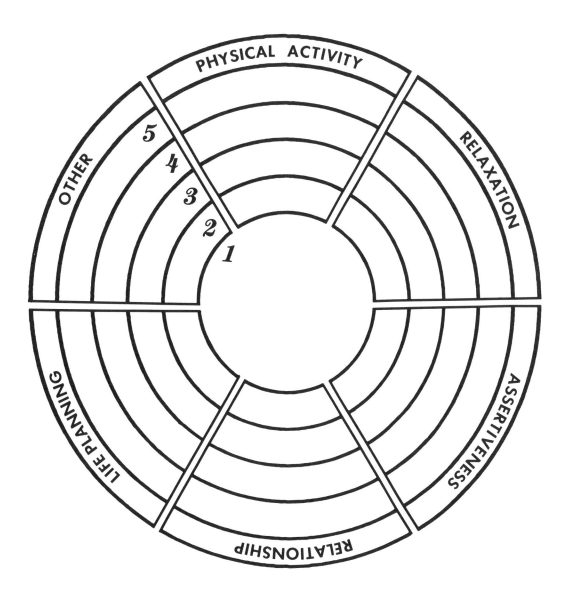

1. Undifferentiated Awareness = "don't know—doesn't apply"
2. Heightened Awareness = "know a little—may be relevant"
3. Personal Awareness = "know a lot—it's important to me"
4. Proactive Awareness = "value these skills—use some of them"
5. Internalized Awareness = "value skills highly—use regularly"

STUDENT COURSE SYLLABUS

Welcome to this course. In the next twelve sessions we'll be exploring various skills that we consider necessary for life in "the jungle." This syllabus is your itinerary for the trip; don't lose it! All the information you need about goals, session topics, homework, and final projects is in this packet. If you'd like further information on any of the areas and skills presented in the course, check the references in *Fighting Invisible Tigers*, or with your teacher.

Goals

The overall aim of the course is to help you increase your awareness of stress—what it is, where it comes from, how you handle it—and your stress management skills. The seven specific goals are to enable you to:

1. Fully understand and feel the difference between stress and relaxation

2. Understand the psychobiological nature and origins of stress

3. Describe your own physical and emotional response to stress

4. Evaluate your current stress level and methods for coping

5. Recognize the difference between coping (just getting by) and proactive stress management

6. Feel the benefit of a range of lifeskills

7. Practice five types of lifeskills

Session Schedule

Topic	Date	Place
1. Orientation to Lifeskills		
2. Life in the Jungle		
3. Coping vs. Stress Management		
4. Getting Physical		
5. The Eye of the Hurricane		
6. Communication Styles		
7. Being Assertive		
8. Friendship Levels		
9. Weaving a Safety Net		
10. Scripting the Future		
11. Planning for Change		
12. Moving On		

Homework Assignments

(All readings are from *Fighting Invisible Tigers: A Stress Management Guide For Teens*)

Date Due

Session 1: Pages 1-25

Session 2: Pages 27-40
Student inventory on stress

Session 3: Pages 41-55

Session 4: Pages 55-66
Student inventory of physical activity

Session 5: Pages 67-76
Student inventory on relaxation skills

Session 6: Student inventory on assertiveness

Session 7: Pages 77-86

Session 8: Student inventory on relationship skills

Session 9: Pages 87-102

Session 10: Student inventory on planning skills

Session 11: Pages 103-114

Final Projects

There are two final projects due on the last session (#12). These are: (1) a relaxation audio tape that you script, direct, and record yourself; and (2) a three-to-five page personal growth plan. You will begin to work on these projects approximately halfway through the course.

The relaxation audio tape can be made on any tape recorder that plays cassettes. You'll be learning about (and practicing) relaxation skills in the course, so this will give you an idea of what a tape is or can be. Later on, you'll get an instruction sheet that explains materials, procedures, and evaluation criteria in detail.

Similarly, the growth plan will be a personalized contract with yourself (and perhaps another person) to keep working on one area of lifeskills after the course is over. Another more detailed instruction sheet on this will be coming later in the course.

Session 2

LIFE IN THE JUNGLE

Overview

Stress is a biologically inherited response of humans to any potentially threatening or challenging stimuli. The "fight or flight response" consists of a chain of psychological and physiological events; it can be provoked by "cognitions" (i.e., thoughts, fears, memories) as well as physical danger. In a group discussion, students comment on the signs of stress they notice in people around them, and discuss the societal norms (such as the emphasis on winning in sports) that create stress. Significant events that cause stress are discussed in this session, as well as the relationship between stress level and performance.

Learner Outcomes

The purpose of the session is to enable students to:

1. Describe the nature and origins of stress

2. Identify symptoms of stress in human beings

3. Identify the cultural norms surrounding the management of stress

4. Explain why certain life events might be considered universally stressful

5. Explain the relationship between stress levels and performance

Agenda

In order to achieve these outcomes, teachers need to:

1. Present an overview of the definition and nature of stress (15 min.)

2. Lead a group discussion in which students identify common stress signals in others, and the cultural norms regarding stress (15 min.)

3.   Present an overhead and discuss the relationship between stress levels and performance (10 min.)

4.   Assign homework

Resources and Materials

1.   Ten Most Stressful Life Events (see page 43)

2.   Relationship of Stress Level to Performance (see page 44)

3.   Student Inventory on Stress (see page 45)

4.   Overhead projector and screen

5.   Blackboard or easel pad

Activities

1.   Overview of stress

Ask students how they would define stress; see if they can recall and elaborate upon the material read for homework. Differentiate between a *stressor,* which is the event, person, or task (the "tiger") which incites stress and the emotional and physical sensations of stress. What we typically call stress is the response to "any action or situation that places special physical or psychological demands on us."[1] In order for the physiological/psychological response to occur, we have to mentally *perceive* the stressor as dangerous. The more dangerous we perceive a situation to be, and less able we feel to control or prepare for it, the greater our stress response.

Describe what's happening to the body during acute stress by explaining the fight or flight syndrome. Some of the key points in this syndrome are:[2]

■   a stress-related neurochemical called noradrenaline is released in the nucleus of the brainstem

■   the noradrenaline quickly travels throughout the brain's branching nerve fibers and into the spinal cord

■   the sympathetic nerve cells of the nervous system accelerate the heart beat and stimulate the adrenal glands, which in turn produce more adrenaline that circulates the blood faster.

■   as the heart speeds up, the body heats up, resulting in perspiration, rapid breathing, increased energy reserves, and muscular tension

Ask students why this response might be useful to cave dwellers and animals. How would these physical changes prepare someone to either fight or flee? How useful is this type of physiological response to us today? Give examples.

Some interesting research on stress indicates that several factors affect our perception of the severity of stress, other than the awesomeness of the "tiger" itself. Two of the most significant of these factors are whether a person (1) feels any control over the amount or type of stress, or (2) receives any advance warning of danger or pain. Control over the source of stress appears to delay or prevent people from disintegrating under pressure. Similarly, being able to predict or prepare for stress enhances a person's stability during stress.

Although most of the research in this area has been conducted on laboratory animals, one study of human subjects deserves mention:[3]

> ■ Believing that the degree of control an executive has over the organization serves as a buffer against stress, and that subordinates are more likely to suffer from ulcers, headaches, or high blood pressure because of their lack of control, the Metropolitan Life Insurance Company studied 1,078 top executives in Fortune 500 companies in 1974. They found these executives' "mortality rate was 37 percent *lower* than that of other men of the same ages." This came somewhat as a surprise, for "type A" leaders (such as corporate executives) had been thought to suffer more from stress than "type B" followers. This study suggests that degree of control over stress worked in the top manager's favor.

Interestingly enough, researchers in the health professions have begun to look seriously at the relationship of illness to stress only in recent decades. Intuitively, the connection appears obvious; a body in constant stimulation, preparing for battle or flight, is repeatedly draining itself of vital resources, and thus has fewer resources with which to protect itself from disease. Professionals in nearly every health field, from nursing to internal medicine to psychiatry to dentistry to nutritional science, are exploring these correlations.

Currently, stress is believed to be a major factor in coronary artery disease, stomach ulcers, colitis, chronic backaches, headaches, and muscular tension. Two very stressful situations, the death of a spouse or the onset of a serious depression, are "associated with an increased risk of cancer in humans."[4] Because stress depletes the body's resources, it lowers the body's resistance both to cold viruses and more serious infectious diseases like pneumonia. Prolonged stress weakens the body's entire immune system, and may trigger or exacerbate illnesses such as cancer, multiple sclerosis, diabetes, and rheumatoid arthritis. Stress contributes to the eating disorders of obesity, bulimia, anorexia, and to alcoholism and drug addiction. With its accompanying hormonal secretions, stress is even believed to be a prime contributor to acne flare-ups![5]

2. Identify stress symptoms in others

Discuss the individual nature of people's reactions to stressors. The sensation of stress is actually an internal phenomenon. Different triggers incite stress in different people. A math test for one of us may be mildly unpleasant, for you it may be exciting, for someone else it may be horrendous. People do different things with their stress. Some confront it and look for solutions, some get wild and crazy (hyper). Others sit tight, real quiet and tense, others get angry and find someone to blame. Some people stutter, others get bossy and irritable.

Ask students to think how someone they know acts when he or she is stressed. How does that person's stress show? What do they do? List the symptoms on the board. Ask the student why he or she thinks the named behaviors (i.e., wild exhuberance, overeating, arguing, becoming withdrawn) signify stress.

This discussion indirectly prepares students to consider their own stressors, their own stress symptoms, their own patterns or cycles of stress. Our method calls for working up to personal assessment slowly. Unless the group is especially open and verbal about personal issues, it will be easier for students to analyze other people's stress signals before analyzing their own. Similarly, in the exercise below, it will be easier for them to talk about common life events that cause stress, rather than the specific events troubling them in their own lives. The self-inventory given as a homework assignment at the end of the sessions engages students more directly in personal assessment.

3. Stressful life events

Even though people react differently to stress, some life events are known to be difficult even for the calmest, most stoic, or even-keeled person. Ask students if they believe in universally stressful events. If so, does that mean as human beings we have similar needs? Are we vulnerable to the same kinds of pain? Present the overhead of 10 Most Stressful Life Events, and explain that they were generated by researchers who were studying adults. Consequently, the list may not reflect what's stressful for students like them. Also, the list doesn't take into account the interactive nature of stressors: a parking ticket on the same day as a big exam and dinner with a newly divorced parent adds up to more stress than it would on a happier day. An interesting thing to draw students attention to is that both so-called happy events (e.g., marriage, birth of a child) are listed as well as unhappy events (e.g., death, divorce) as sources of stress. Ask students to comment on this.

40

| 4. | Relationship of stress level to performance | Although the extra power and heat caused by the fight or flight response enabled the cave dweller to fight more aggressively, or flee more successfully, today "many components of the stress response in humans work to shorten rather than lengthen a person's life span."[6] |

Show students the overhead illustrating the relationship between stress and performance. Explain that the term "performance" here applies to any general category of performance, such as sports, intellectual (school), musical, or dramatic performances. In moderate or controlled amounts, stress can help us perform at our best. It arouses us, increases our alertness, provides us with energy. As stress and anxiety mount to an intolerable level, however, our performance begins to disintegrate. A sense of fatigue, disorganization, inattention takes over, making concentration, physical coordination, even visual perception difficult. The ability to take in any new information or to remember previously learned material is particularly affected when we're under too much stress.

Ask students to turn to the person next to them and for the next two minutes, to discuss what it feels like to have "stress overload."

5. Homework

Hand out the Student Inventory on Stress to complete for next time. Explain that the inventories are numbered but anonymous, and that students should remember their number. You'll be handing back the six completed inventories on the last day of class. They won't be graded, but they are required. (Remember to number the inventories ahead of time. Then, check students off a list when they hand in their completed inventories. In this way, you'll have a record of who's completed their homework assignments.)

The reading assignment is for pages 27-40 in *Fighting Invisible Tigers*.

Alternative Suggestions

As an alternative to discussing the origins and nature of stress in a lecture format, show the film "Stress and the Emotions" from the Public Broadcasting System series *The Brain*. (You'll have to contact PBS or your local public television station.) This is an hour-long segment, so some pre-screening and partial showing will probably be necessary.

If a science teacher or psychologist is one of the co-teachers, he or she could contribute many more examples of the research being conducted on the stress response itself, and on the effects of stress on psychological and physical health.

References

[1]Restak, R. *The Brain.* New York: Bantam Books, 1984.

[2]Ibid.

[3]Ibid.

[4]Ibid.

[5]Hamilton, E. and Whitney, E. *Nutrition: Concepts and Controversy.* St. Paul (Mn): West Publishing Company, 1979.

[6]Restak, R. *The Brain.* New York: Bantam Books, 1984.

TEN MOST STRESSFUL LIFE EVENTS

1. Death of spouse or loved one (immediate family)

2. Divorce

3. Marital separation

4. Death of a close family member

5. Major personal injury or illness

6. Marriage

7. Being fired or laid off work

8. Major change in health or behavior of family member

9. Sexual difficulties

10. Gaining a new family member

Excerpt from *The Life Event Scale*, a measure developed by Dr. Thomas Holmes and Dr. Richard Raahe. See Richard Restak, *The Brain*. New York: Bantam Books, 1984.

RELATIONSHIP OF STRESS LEVEL TO PERFORMANCE

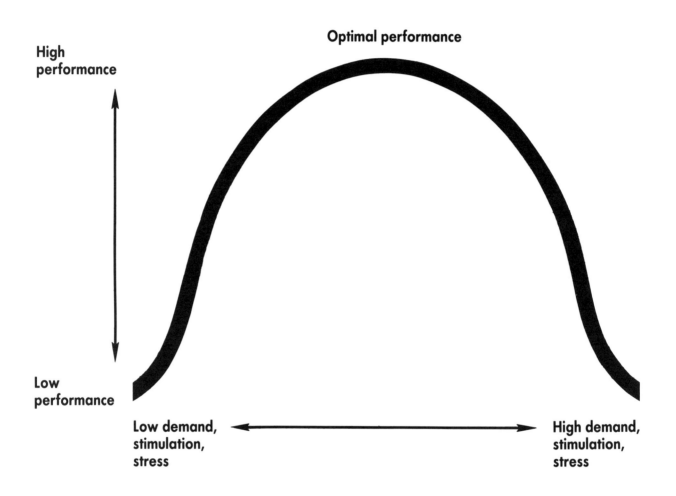

Performance = intellectual, athletic, artistic, musical, interpersonal, or other

STUDENT INVENTORY
ON STRESS

1. Begin by thinking back over the past 24 hours in your life. Try to "see" these hours spread out like a timeline, beginning with yesterday at this very hour, continuing through the day and evening, through the night, into the early morning, and on to today's activities. When, during these hours, were you under stress? Under the most stress? When were you relaxed, the most relaxed?

2. Mark off these different hours of peace and stress in your mind's eye, or on a sheet of paper if you prefer. Are you often stressed or relaxed during these same time periods? Is there a daily pattern, or is it just random?

3. How can you tell that you're stressed? What does your body feel like during your most stressed period(s)? How do you feel emotionally during stressful periods?

4. How do you interact with other people during these different periods? What language—verbal or body or both—do you use when you're stressed? What does your face look like? How does your voice sound?

5. List three major stressors in your life.

6. What do you do when you're reaching your limits?

7. If you were to offer a good friend some advice on managing stress, what would you say?

8. These thoughts contain valuable information about yourself. These are personal signs of stress, personal signs of peace. Don't throw this information away. You'll need to be aware of these symptoms, so you can learn to manage them.

Session 3

COPING VS. STRESS MANAGEMENT

Overview

When people haven't identified the triggers that distress them, or the habits they unconsciously perpetuate that increase stress, they're unlikely to feel prepared or confident when sudden challenges arise. Instead they react somewhat reflexively, turning (out of habit) to short-term strategies that distract them or dull the pain.

Coping is a natural survival mechanism. Some coping strategies are healthful and positive, but the essence of even positive coping is the avoidance of feeling; the root causes of stress are never addressed. Too much coping can be destructive and lead to a "crashing and burning" style of existence. In this session, long-term management skills are contrasted with positive and negative coping strategies, and students construct their own lists of "most stressful events."

Learner Outcomes

The purpose of this session is to enable students to:

1. Differentiate between coping and stress management

2. Identify positive and negative coping strategies

3. Identify the cultural norms surrounding coping strategies

4. Identify life events that are stressful for students

5. Compare the sensation of stress with that of relaxation

Agenda

In order to accomplish these outcomes, teachers need to:

1. Lead a group discussion on the misconceptions people have about stress and the difference between coping and stress management (15 min.)

2. Coordinate a small group activity in which students list and discuss the ten most stressful life events for teens (20 min.)

3. Conduct a progressive relaxation exercise (15 min.)

4. Collect student inventories on stress and assign homework.

Resources and Materials

1. Ten Most Stressful Life Events for Students (See page 54)

2. Carpeted classroom or gym with mats

3. Blackboard or easel pad

Activities

1. Group discussion on coping vs. stress management

To begin discussion, ask students if they can recall any of the twelve misconceptions listed in ***Fighting Invisible Tigers*** (p. 29). Typical misconceptions or reactions to stress are: "It's not okay to cry." "I must be crazy to think or feel the way I do." "If I can just get through today, tomorrow will be better." Ask students:

■ What are some typical (mis)conceptions people have about stress? Knowing what you know now about stress, what messages or attitudes around you seem to be mistaken?

(List on board)

■ What messages do students get from society (i.e., television and radio media, advertising, their parents, neighbors, and community) about what to do with stress?

■ What coping patterns (such as distraction, avoidance, escape) are sanctioned by our culture? What patterns are unacceptable? Why or why not?

48

- Does anyone know how stress is handled in foreign countries, or in primitive cultures? (If there are foreign students or students with strong ethnic traditions in the class, ask them if they would like to comment on this.)

- Why are some of these messages from society on stress "misconceptions?" What is gained by thinking *this*, for example (point to misconception on board), is it true? What is lost?

- What's the difference between coping strategies and stress management (lifeskills?)

- What happens when we try to cope, day to day, but never get to the source of the stress?

- Where can we find support for decisions to learn lifeskills?

Summarize the common forms of coping listed on pages 32-40 in ***Fighting Invisible Tigers*** under distractions, avoidance, and escape. Typical distractions include watching television, eating, taking a bath, reading a book. Distractions are pretty harmless but also the shortest-lived and least potent method of coping. Avoidance tactics are distractions in the extreme: constantly wearing earphones (even during class or suppertime) is an example. Avoidance tactics usually allow the problem to become bigger, which triggers more avoidance, thus becoming a vicious circle. Excessive sleep, procrastination, even illness, can be signs of avoidance. Escapist behaviors are distraction and avoidance measures taken to the extreme. They are a signal that the limits of coping have been reached, and the person wants "out." Skipping school, running away from home, and abusing drugs or alcohol are means of escape with serious consequences.

Ask students to suggest varying coping behaviors and then to classify them into the appropriate category of positive or negative coping. Repeat that stress is something that occurs *inside* of each person even though it may be triggered by events or pressures from the outside. How people respond to stress is often conditioned—first by the prevailing habits in a person's family, and (second) by social norms as conveyed by neighbors, schools, and the media. Indicate that we don't always get immediate support from people around us to use lifeskills, but that we can learn to create that support. (More about that in Sessions 8 and 9.)

As you go through this discussion, you may encounter some confusion over the concept of "misconceptions." Misconceptions are the ill-formed or unrealistic notions we have about the nature or origins of

49

stress and the so-called "proper" ways to deal with stress. Misconceptions often point to negative coping strategies, and in the group discussion your list of "misconceptions" may spill over to include "coping strategies." Actually, a misconception (e.g., "It's not okay to cry") leads to an inadequate strategy (e.g., holding everything in and denying the pain).

You may similarly need to clarify the difference between positive and negative coping strategies. Positive methods of "quick relief" include going for a walk after an argument at home; doing some relaxation or deep breathing before an exam; getting rid of tension by doing some physical activity. Examples of negative coping strategies can include tactics like those listed above, but done to the extreme. Walking for six hours in the dead of night, meditating before every class, or jogging seven days a week for three hours a day—these are signs that coping strategies are being pushed to unreasonable limits. Over-intellectualizing or rationalizing a problem can also do more harm than good if it constitutes a person's prevailing method of stress management. Finally, certain coping strategies (e.g., drinking, drugs) quickly become destructive as well as ineffective.

2. Small group activity

First, arrange students into small groups of three to four people. Use your own method for forming groups, or try this technique: ask every student whose birthday falls in the spring (March, April, May) to meet in one corner of the room. People with summer birthdays (June, July, August) meet in another corner. Split up fall and winter birthdays similarly. Then, distribute the student worksheet "Ten Most Stressful Life Events to Student," one per group, and give them the following instructions.

Ten Most Stressful Life Events for Students

Last week we looked at one research team's list of the ten most stressful life events for adults. Do you remember what some of those events were? Okay, in the next twenty minutes, I'd like each group to decide which life events are the most stressful for teens. Don't worry about thinking too far into the future, just list the events that typically cause people your age a lot of trauma. These events don't have to have happened to you. Talk about which events qualify and why. Then vote on which are the most stressful, and re-list the events in order of priority from most to least stressful. Elect a leader or scribe to write down your final answers. Here's a worksheet to write on.

After students complete the activity, collect all the worksheets. You'll be compiling their responses and posting the class's final list on a bulletin board next week.

3. Relaxation exercise

If possible, have students lie down on the floor for another progressive relaxation exercise. This exercise is a variation of the one conducted in Session 1. Its purpose is to reinforce the skills of relaxation and to help students relieve tension and enjoy the class. This exercise also gets them accustomed to the process of letting go, which should make it easier for them to do the meditation and exercise in Session 5.

Progressive Relaxation Script

Begin by lying on your back with your eyes closed, hands at your sides, facing upwards. Let your feet fall apart naturally as you begin to breathe slowly and deeply. Take a long, deep inhalation, then release it with a sign. You're starting to let go of all your tension, you're going to allow yourself to relax.

As your body relaxes, you begin to feel gravity pressing you into the floor. Under your heels, calves, and thighs you'll feel the weight of your legs. Under your buttocks, back, shoulders, and arms, the feeling of weight is pressing down. The floor will support you. Your head becomes heavier and heavier as the muscles in the back of your neck and face relax, soften, and release. Your whole body is heavy and relaxed, with the floor doing all the work of supporting. Gravity does the work as the body lets go and allows itself to rest completely. Your mind is very alert. The body is resting quietly. Be still now, focus on your breathing; breathe through your nose in long, steady breaths.

Become aware of your hands now—first your right hand, then your left hand. Slowly let each hand tighten into a fist. Be careful to tense only the muscles in your hands and arms. Make those fists tight, but keep your face relaxed; your stomach and shoulders are loose. Tighter, tighter, as tight as possible, hold all the tension in those two fists; feel all the work—all the energy that's required to hold in that tension.

Now slowly relax your hands. Feel the tension gradually leaving your fingers. Feel your arms and hands loosening and softening. Continue to say (silently) to yourself, "Let go, relax; let go, relax," even after you have uncurled your hands and can no longer feel any tightness. Open your hands wide in a stretch, then allow them to return to a "normal" position. As your arms and hands again become heavy and relaxed, experience the difference between the work of holding, and the naturalness of letting go.

51

Lying still, body relaxed and calm, slowly tighten the muscles in your face. Tighten the muscles around your eyes, your forehead, your jaw, your mouth. Feel your expression scrunch up hard, getting tight, getting as tight as possible. It's uncomfortable, but just for a moment feel this tension and the cost in energy. Feel your lips and teeth. Your eyes, scalp, throat, and especially your forehead are aching, they're working so hard. Make sure the tension is contained just in the face, that the shoulder and stomach muscles are relaxed.

Ever so slowly and gradually, begin to release. Learn to experience tension leaving the muscles. Release this tension slowly saying to yourself, "Let go, relax." Forehead and eyes let go; mouth, jaw and scalp relax. Let go and relax, even after you can no longer feel any tightness in your face. The muscles in your face are soft and relaxed again. Your head is heavy and relaxed. Take a deep breath and exhale slowly, releasing any leftover tension. Another deep inhalation and long, slow exhalation, letting relaxation spread through your whole body.

Now pull your shoulders up toward your head. Take a deep inhalation and hold it, then tighten your stomach and back. Hold this tension. Your breathing will be shallow, but hold it. Make your shoulders, chest, stomach, and back as tight as possible. Again be sure to contain the tension in these areas only. Your face, arms and hands, legs should remain calm and relaxed. Experience the tension in the trunk of your body. Make it tighter, tighter. Notice the difficulty with your breathing. This is how many people unknowingly carry tension in their bodies. Notice how much work is required to maintain this tightness, this unpleasant tension.

Again now, slowly release this tension, as slowly as you can. Feel the tension leaving your shoulders, your chest, your stomach, your back. Say to yourself, "Let go, relax; let go, relax." Feel the process of letting go, the return of natural breathing, the loosening and softening of your muscles. Keep letting go, even after your body feels relaxed. Take a long deep breath, then release it. No tensions now, just quiet. Focus on your breath.

On your next inhalation, let your buttocks begin to tighten along with your legs. Tighten your thighs and calves. Point your toes hard so your legs are rigid. Make the muscles in your seat and legs hard, but keep your face, shoulders, and other areas relaxed. Make your breathing soft and natural as you hold this tension in your lower body. Feel the tension in your feet, calves, thighs, and buttocks get tighter and tighter.

Ever so slowly, allow the tension to release a little at a time. Experience varying degrees of tension as you continue to release, saying to yourself, "Let go, relax." Feel your buttocks and thighs and calves and feet releasing, your toes come up into a more normal position. Take a deep breath, hold it, then release, letting go of any remaining tension in your body. Again experience the heaviness in your body. Completely let go and feel waves of relaxation with each breath. Like a gentle, warm ocean wave that washes over you, starting from the soles of your feet up to head and back, these waves of calmness and peace spread over you.

Remember how much work and discomfort there was in holding. Remember how restful and natural letting go was. Experience this calm in your body now. Remember what this place is like, to make your return easier. Quietly, focus on your breath now, the sound and sensation of your breath passing. Thoughts may come but do not attach to them; decide to stay focused on your breath. Your body is quiet; your mind is alert.

Prepare to return now by taking control of your breath. Make your breath stronger and quicker with each inhalation. Imagine with each breath that you're bringing fresh, positive energy into your body. With each exhalation, you're releasing old, tired energy. Feel the energy you've created flowing through your body, going down into your fingertips, going down to your toes. Another deep inhalation and move this new energy into your face, allowing your eyes to open and a smile to grow. One more deep inhalation, sit up, smile. The exercise has ended.

4. Homework

Assign students pages 41-55 in *Fighting Invisible Tigers*.

Alternate Suggestions

Again, audio relaxation tapes or other relaxation exercises may be substituted for the script presented here. Additionally, you may wish to bring in a guest teacher (e.g., yoga instructor or other relaxation educator) to demonstrate a relaxation technique.

TEN MOST STRESSFUL LIFE EVENTS FOR STUDENTS

Suggested Events	Number Votes	Priority
1.		
2.		
3.		
4.		
5.		
6.		
7.		
8.		
9.		
10.		
Other:		

Session 4

GETTING PHYSICAL

Overview

With this session, the course emphasis shifts from understanding the nature and origin of stress to the description and practice of five lifeskills. The lifeskill addressed in this session is "physical activity." Physical activity differs from competitive sports and (some) exercise routines, both of which can build bodies, but also create terrific mental, physical, and emotional strain. When approached with the right mind set, physical activity can be a very effective, primary way to release stored tension and to improve the body's overall machinery. An efficient body handles the psychophysical demands of stress more effectively. It also burns fat, reduces (or redistributes) weight, and maintains overall physical health and strength.

In this session students learn the basic principles of aerobic exercise, and participate in an activity in which their training heart rates are determined. They also generate *appropriate* activity prescriptions for themselves.

Learner Outcomes

The purpose of this session is to enable students to:

1. Identify the cultural norms surrounding physical activity

2. Distinguish between the relaxation (i.e., the body during a resting state) and physical activity (i.e., the body at a training rate of activity)

3. Generate a personal activity prescription that takes into account appropriate intensity, duration, and frequency

55

Agenda

In order to accomplish these outcomes, teachers need to:

1. Hand out instructions on the growth plan (the final project) and answer questions (10 min.)

2. Discuss the cultural norms surrounding physical activity (10 min.)

3. Conduct an aerobic exercise in which students determine their resting, training, and maximum heart rates (15 min.)

4. Demonstrate how to apply the FIT formula (15 min.)

5. Post the summary list from Session 3 on Student's Ten Most Stressful Life Events on a bulletin board, and assign homework.

Resources and Materials

1. Final Project Instruction Sheet: Student Growth Plan (see pages 61-62)

2. Target Heart Rate Worksheet (see page 63)

3. Physical Activities That Reduce Stress (see page 64)

4. Student Inventory on Physical Activity (see page 65)

5. A large, somewhat empty classroom or gym with floor mats

6. Stopwatch or clock with second hand

7. Jump ropes (single person ropes)

8. Record or tape of music with steady, moderate beat (optional)

Activities

1. Review Growth Plans

Begin the session by saying that it takes time to change one's life style or habits. When doing so, it helps to have reinforcement and support from others. Generally, the more difficult the behavior change, the greater the need for support and reinforcement. Talk about the growth contract as an opportunity to change in a supportive atmosphere. Hand out the instruction sheet on growth contracts and tell students to begin thinking about which lifeskill area they'd like to work on for their final assignment. Explain that you'll be discussing five lifeskill areas during the next eight sessions. Students are free to develop a growth contract in any of these lifeskills or in an area of their own choosing. The bibliography at the end of the book will provide leads for you and the students.

2. Discuss the cultural norms surrounding physical activity

Ask students to join you in thinking about the reasons why people do—and don't—keep themselves physically active in this culture. Many people in our country lead very sedentary lives. Why? Today, physical activity is almost always synonymous with sports. Why? Ask students about the "messages" they hear about:

■ Who should play games?

■ Who should play competitive sports?

■ What are the options if you don't want to play competitive sports?

■ What does a healthy body look like for women/girls?

■ What does a healthy body look like for men/boys?

■ What's so "good" about being physically fit?

■ How are people supposed to stay physically fit?

■ How hard should you work out to get fit? Is the process supposed to be pleasant or painful?

3. Determine resting, training, and maximum heart rates

Explain that aerobics is just one form of physical activity, but that it serves as a good illustration of how physical movement can release stored tension and be healthful in other ways. "Aerobic" means air, and aerobic exercise is "steady exercise that demands an uninterrupted output from your muscles over a twelve-minute period."[1] An increase in heart rate during physical activity is an indirect measure of how hard the muscles are working. The main criterion for aerobics, then, is continuous and steady activity that maintains a person's heart rate at the proper "training level." As the body exercises aerobically, fat is combusted, muscles increase their strength and change their shape. So aerobics not only releases tension, it improves overall body conditioning.

Any number of physical activities can reduce stored tension, which is good for stress management. Recall that the fight or flight response (stress) prepares the body for action. Even if the body doesn't engage in action (i.e., fight or flee), the person still experiences the physical

57

preparation for it. The physical results of nonreleased tension are restlessness, anxiety, physical tension. Unreleased tension gets expressed by constantly tapping fingers or toes, constant motion, or by the urgent feelings "I've got to get out of here," or "I've got to get going." This energy is physical in nature and needs release.

Although strenuous physical activity can cause injuries and general wear and tear, a moderate amount releases tension and creates a degree of relaxation. One way to determine the right kind and amount of physical activity for yourself is the FIT formula, which is described in *Fighting Invisible Tigers* on pages 45-47. This formula operates on the principles of aerobics. You're going to experience this approach today in an exercise.

Script For Determining Heart Rates

(Based on the approach developed by Covert Bailey)

Please circulate this "Target Heart Rate Worksheet." First, we're going to determine your resting heart rate by taking your pulse for six seconds. To find your pulse, place your index and middle fingers (not thumb) either on your wrist near the thumb, or neck along side of the Adam's apple. Everyone have it? Okay, you're going to count the number of beats while I time you. Starting counting . . . now! Okay, stop! How many beats did you get? Let's do it one more time and get it as exact as you can. Multiply that number by ten and record it on your worksheet under "Resting Heart Rate."

Next, to calculate your maximum heart rate, subtract your age from 220, then list the remainder on the worksheet. Good! Finally, to find your training heart rate, look on the table on your worksheet. Find your maximum heart rate on one of the rows going down the left hand side of the table, and your resting heart rate among the column headers at the top. Your "target" heart rate is in the square that matches this row and column. This number represents the *maximum* beats per minute for the most beneficial workout.

Now we're going to bring your heart up to this target training rate. First, choose an activity—either jumping rope, power walking, jogging, or dancing, and find a partner who's interested in doing the same activity. When I say begin, start doing the activity together, but talk to each other while you do your activity. **If you can't keep up a conversation, slow down the activity, you're working too hard.**

Make sure your partner doesn't overdo it! Quite likely you'll have different training rates, and will reach your training rates at different paces. We'll do this for a minute or two, then stop to see whether your pulse is within ten points of your training rate. We'll do that by again taking your pulse for six seconds and multiplying that answer by ten. You *must* stop when I say stop and time yourself because your heart will begin to "recover" (slow down) almost immediately.

When the activity is over, explain that what students just experienced was the physical difference between their body's resting state and an active state which represents approximately 60 percent - 70 percent of their maximum heart rate. Pulse level indicates stress, as they've learned through the fight or flight response. The maximum heart rate equals too much stress (it could be lethal, especially when they are older), and is not considered a good pace for any sport or exercise. This "training rate" identifies a comfortable level of exercise (stress) for achieving aerobic conditioning. Working harder than this rate doesn't greatly increase the benefit gained from the activity.

When you do the aerobic exercise, make sure you look out for students who are overweight, who have a physical handicap or disability, or for anyone whom you suspect is out of shape. Students will naturally try to keep up with each other, but one partner's pace may be too intense for the other. Some very fit students may need to exercise twice as hard as others to get their heart rate up to the training level. Others may raise it sufficiently just by walking vigorously. Make sure you counsel students to choose an activity that feels comfortable and can be sustained for five minutes. If they can't talk to each other, or whistle or sing (softly) while doing the exercise, they're probably working too hard.

4. Demonstrate how to apply the FIT formula

Pass around the student handout listing various physical activities. Share with students (our) philosophy that we needn't be superstars to enjoy and use our bodies. The trick is to find the right activity (or, variety of activities), the right **F**requency, the right **I**ntensity level and the right amount of **T**ime for the activity.

Ask a student to volunteer a preferred activity. Problem-solve with that student how he or she might be able to engage in that (and other) activities in ways that would release tension and promote fitness. For example, if they like to ride bikes, riding bikes for about a half hour, three times a week, maintaining a steady rate without getting short of breath, is an appropriate activity prescription for them.

Ask students what obstacles they encounter when trying to use physical activity routinely as a stress reducer: Is it their own lack of interest? Cost of equipment? Lack of a friend to do it with? Time or other obligations? Problem-solve one or two of these obstacles. Suggest some ways people might creatively choose or alter an activity, combine it with another task, or schedule it with a friend.

Examples:

- Power-walk the mall before shopping.

- Join a water ballet class rather than speed swimming.

- Do a different aerobic exercise each week to prevent boredom.

- Make a 12-minute tape of favorite music and dance every afternoon after school.

- Play co-ed soccer for fun, and don't keep score.

- Play any mixed-age team sports (e.g., soccer, volleyball) and don't keep score.

5. Post list and assign homework

Invite students to look at the final, summary list of their Ten Most Stressful Life Events for Students that you've posted on the board. Then, assign them the inventory on physical exercise, and pages 55-66 in *Fighting Invisible Tigers*.

Alternative Suggestions

Invite the physical education teacher, or local aerobics teacher to co-teach this session if you prefer not to lead the aerobic exercise yourself. Choose some lively music to accompany the exercise to make the atmosphere fun.

References

[1]Bailey, C. *Fit or Fat?* Boston: Houghton Mifflin Company, 1977.

Final Project Instruction Sheet

STUDENT GROWTH PLAN

This project gives you an opportunity to:

a. Practice the lifeskill of clarifying your values, interests, and goals

b. Practice the lifeskill of problem-solving, of constructing a plan to achieve a goal

c. Develop a plan you can implement after the course is over, and therefore achieve a short-term goal

---

The assignment is to select a lifeskill area (i.e., physical activity, relaxation, assertiveness, relationship, life planning, or your own particular area), prepare a three-to-five page paper that outlines specific goals you'd like to achieve in this area, and strategies for achieving those goals. At a minimum, your plan should include the following:

1. Title and description of lifeskill area

- specific activities within that area (e.g., a plan for regular and reasonable physical activity)

- reasons why you chose this area, these activities

- your previous experience with or feelings towards this activity

2. Long-term and short-term goals

- future or long-range goals you'd like to accomplish in this lifeskill area (two or three years on down the road, or even more)

- immediate goal that can be accomplished in the near future (within one or two months, or within the school year, for example)

- Target deadline for short-term goal

3. A definition or measure of successful completion of goal

■ specific degree or level of success that you would be satisfied with, or range of degrees

4. List of potential resources

■ key decision-makers

■ people who can help (friends, teachers, parents)

■ community resources (library, museums, etc.)

5. List of potential constraints or problems

■ personal limitations or roadblocks

■ external limitations or roadblocks

6. Tentative solutions to anticipated difficulties

■ special types of reinforcements or rewards to use when motivation is lagging

■ people from your support network who will hold you to your commitments

■ other

You'll have time to work on this plan with your peers in small groups during the next-to-last session of the course. Start thinking about which lifeskill area you'd like to develop. There are extra bonus points for those of you who choose one of your less well-developed lifeskill areas.

The criteria on which I'll be evaluating your growth plans are:

1. Meaningful (sincere) short-term and long-term goals

2. A reasonable measure of success has been defined

3. A realistic and reasonable plan is proposed

4. Evidence that problems have been anticipated and tentative solutions explored

5. Evidence that resources, including people, have been identified

6. Personal reinforcements have been defined

7. Extra bonus point for multiple strategies, multiple resources, and especially thoughtful solutions to anticipated problems

TARGET HEART RATE WORKSHEET

Resting Heart Rate

To calculate your resting heart rate, take your pulse for exactly six seconds. Multiply your answer by ten. If the number of beats is between two whole numbers, multiply the lower number by ten, then add five for your answer.

Resting Heart Rate = _____

Maximum Heart Rate

To determine your maximum heart rate, subtract your age from 220.

Maximum Heart Rate = _____

Training ("Target") Heart Rate*

Locate your maximum heart rate in the rows down the left hand side of the table, and your resting heart rate among the headers across the columns on the top. Your target rate (beats per minute) is listed where the row and column meet.

Maximum Heart Rate	Resting Heart Rate				
	50	**55**	**60**	**65**	**70**
210	186.5	191.5	196.5	201.5	206.5
209	185	191	196	200	206
208	185	190	195	200	205
207	184.5	189.5	194.5	199.5	204.5
206	184	189	194	199	204
205	183	188	193	198	203
204	182.5	187.5	192.5	197.5	202.5
203	182	187	192	197	202

(Numbers have been rounded off to nearest .50).

*1. Can divide by 6 for a 10 second count.

2. More important than the actual number is how you feel doing your activity. Getting fit doesn't have to be uncomfortable. If you are out of breath or feel discomfort, you are overdoing it.

PHYSICAL ACTIVITIES
THAT CAN REDUCE STRESS

gymnastics frisbee-ing bowling tennis kayaking rowing roller skating snowshoeing boxing football jogging ice skating surfing soccer wood chopping lacrosse basketball bicycling golf snow skiing baseball jumping rope field hockey wrestling dancing handball racquetball ice hockey weightlifting squash swimming volleyball martial arts skate boarding Ping-Pong juggling track badminton yoga mime isometrics croquet softball canoeing hiking power walking horseback riding

Some of these activities are much better stress-reducers than others; can you explain why? Which might work best for you? How could you make more of these activities fun and relaxing for you?

STUDENT INVENTORY ON PHYSICAL ACTIVITY

1. The words "physical exercise" and "sports" conjure up different emotions for different people. To some kids, for example, physical education is the best (and perhaps only) good thing about school. They simply *have* to move around; sitting still is torture. To others, physical education is the worst part of their day. Everything remotely related to sports and exercise is frustrating, boring, or embarrassing. Too often, kids and adults live in the shadow of athletes with heroic status; we feel compelled to compete at their level or sit on the sidelines. Think about what sports and physical activities in general have meant for you. Are they—have they been—important? How so? Why or why not?

2. If you have negative feelings about physical activities, can you remember how moving around, playing in a physical way, felt when you were younger, before formal competition was introduced? Do you have any positive memories of playing, of riding bikes, or sliding down hills? If so, what were they and why were they enjoyable?

3. List a number of physical activities that you have participated in. Compare the feelings you get from two sample activities; for example, describe how you feel after playing tennis, and compare it to how you feel after skateboarding (choose your own activities). Describe both physical and emotional feelings.

4. Which kinds of physical activities are the best for you? Which give you the most pleasure or fun? Why? Which kinds of activities do you enjoy doing the least? Why don't you enjoy them?

5. Is physical activity a regular part of your day? Explain why or why not, and how (if applicable).

6. How would you describe your overall physical condition? Do you feel good about your body in terms of energy, stamina, strength?

7. Most of the chronic health problems in America today are related to lifestyle including lack of exercise. Physical activity doesn't have to be competitive or dreary. Use the information you've gained about yourself here to write a short activity prescription using the FIT formula.

Session 5

THE EYE OF THE HURRICANE

Overview

Physiological and psychological changes occur when the body relaxes as well as when it experiences stress. In contrast to the flight or fight response, the relaxation response is hallmarked by a slower heartbeat, deeper and slower breathing, and the release of muscular tension. Many religious and secular techniques such as prayer, yoga, meditation, progressive relaxation, and autosuggestion induce these changes.

In this session, the relaxation response is described and an exercise in meditation is conducted.

Learner Outcomes

The purpose of this session is to enable students to:

1. Identify the benefits of relaxation exercises

2. Differentiate between the sensations of stress and relaxation

3. Practice meditation

4. Identify the cultural norms surrounding relaxation

Agenda

In order to accomplish these outcomes, teachers need to:

1. Provide some background on the concepts of progressive relaxation, meditation, and their benefits (15 min.)

2. Conduct a meditation exercise (15 min.)

3. Discuss the cultural norms surrounding relaxation (15 min.)

4. Collect student inventories on physical activity, assign homework, and hand out the instruction sheet on relaxation tapes (see pages 74-75)

Resources and Materials

1. Comfortable room with carpet or mat

2. Final Project Instruction Sheet: Relaxation Tape (see pages 61-62)

3. Student Inventory on Relaxation (see page 76)

Activities

1. Discuss concepts of relaxation

As an opener for this discussion, ask students to write down on a sheet of paper one thing they worry about. They needn't sign their names. It can be anything—large or small—some recurring anxiety, fear, or "guilt trip" that is "stuck" on their minds like a broken record. Then tell them to crumple up the paper and come together in the room: on the count of three they're going to throw the balls of paper up in the air. Just for today and for this hour, they're going to let go of that worry or fear. After throwing the balls up in the air, have students go around the room, unwrap the papers, and read the worries and anxieties of their peers. What do students learn from reading their classmates' concerns?

Explain that today's topic is relaxation. Relaxation exercises are structured ways of letting go of worries and tension. You've already done two simple relaxation exercises in earlier sessions; today the concepts behind these exercises are going to be discussed.

Ask students to define relaxation and to explain the difference between a quiet activity, such as reading a book or watching television, and the specific kind of exercise you're discussing here. Clarify that relaxation is a form of "non-doing," "focused rest," "passive attention," "centering." There are many different kinds of relaxation techniques; ask if students recall (from their reading) three characteristics the techniques have in common. As listed in the student text, relaxation techniques:

1. Must be learned, and they must be practiced

2. Induce noticeable, measurable physiological changes

3. Involve a neutral focus of attention (rather than thinking)

68

The two types of relaxation techniques covered in this course are progressive relaxation and meditation. Both of these require disciplined learning and practice because it is not easy to screen out the steady thought processes of the mind, nor is it simple to quiet a tense body. Both techniques also divert the mind from active thinking to nonverbal, sensory experiences.

In our culture, progressive relaxation and meditation are considered positive coping strategies. They are known to help people endure acute anxiety (such as text anxiety, or fear of the dentist's chair) and acute pain (such as natural childbirth). In other cultures, meditation and relaxation exercises play a major part in people's *daily* lives, and for them they become proactive lifeskills.

Typically, progressive relaxation techniques focus a person's attention on such things as breathing slowly and deeply, or releasing a series of muscles in a systematic fashion. They were first developed formally (in western society) by Dr. Edmund Jacobson, a physician who studied muscular tension in the early 1920s.[1] His studies led to progressive relaxation techniques that have been adopted and developed for a range of medical needs including physical therapy, psychotherapy, and childbirth.

Meditation has been a mainstay of both Eastern and Western religious mystics for centuries. In meditation, the body is relaxed (usually in a sitting position), and attention is focused on a neutral visual object (e.g., a blank wall) or sound (e.g., chanting). The mind is alert but detached from intellectual activity.

Both of these techniques produce similar physical responses in the body. In the early 1960s, these physiological changes were studied by Dr. Herbert Benson at Harvard Medical School. Because of these studies, Benson hypothesized that "the relaxation response is the opposite of the fight and flight response."[2] Specifically, Benson found that during relaxation, oxygen consumption decreases by 13 percent, carbon dioxide production decreases by 12 percent, and eleven to sixteen fewer breaths are taken per minute. He also found a correlation between regular relaxation, relatively low blood pressures, decreased heart rates, decreased blood lactate (a waste product of metabolism), and the intensification of Alpha brain waves. Benson continues to find that regular application of relaxation techniques makes people less susceptible to stressors. More noradrenaline (the "stress chemicals" in the brain) are actually required to cause a rise in blood pressure and heart rate in people who relax regularly than in the person who never plans purposeful relaxation. Today, Benson has developed a four-part instructional series on the relaxation response that draws on different historical uses of meditation and relaxation techniques.

Although meditation is embued with rich religious traditions, its primary benefits to some may be in the psychophysical changes it causes. As Zen master Katsuki Sekida explains, "Zen is not in my view a philosophy or mysticism. It is simply a practice of readjustment of nervous activity. That is, it restores the distorted nervous system to its normal functioning."[3]

Have students hypothesize what they expect the benefits of relaxation will be for them. Not many will be needing to lower blood pressure, although some may have some chronic illnesses that benefit from regular relaxation. See how specifically you can encourage them to articulate the anticipated benefits.

2. Meditation exercise

To do the meditation exercise, give students instructions on how to assume the training position and then proceed. For this session, students should only be expected to meditate for a period of ten minutes. The remainder of the allotted time is spent getting set up, and "debriefing" students on their experiences.

Script for Meditation Exercise

Everyone please find a firm chair and turn it towards a blank portion of the wall. Sit as far apart from the next person as possible. Sit facing the wall with your back relaxed but straight. Your feet should be flat on the floor. Fold your hands in your lap or lay them along the tops of your thighs. Keeping your head upright, tuck your chin back and in. Keep your eyes open and look down at about a 45-degree angle. You should be staring at the wall directly in front of you. The purpose here is to align your body so it feels centered—it may seem tiring at first, but over time it is easier because spinal alignment allows the back muscles to be more relaxed. It also allows the diaphragm to expand more fully when breathing, which helps calm and slow the body.

This is the basic training posture. When you assume it, you join a company of meditators all over the world. To do this meditation exercise, maintain this posture in silence and count your breaths. Please breathe through your nose as we learned to do in the previous relaxation exercises. You'll inhale and silently count "one," then exhale and silently count "two," and so on up to ten. When you reach ten, start over again one on with the next inhalation.

There are only four rules to remember:

1. Don't try to manipulate your breathing, just let it come naturally

70

2. Don't move your body

3. Don't stop before I tell you it's time to stop

4. If you get distracted and lose count, go back to one and start again

Common difficulties for first-time meditators include itchy, twitchy bodies and restless minds, feeling silly, losing track of time, forgetting which number they're on, bodily aches and discomfort, even loneliness. Help students understand that this is the restless part of them that resists slowing down. It requires patience and practice to slow the steady stream of activity in one's mind and body. Have students talk about some of the things that interfered with their ability to concentrate, to relax. (Have them also talk about the positive outcomes.)

> **The best technique is not to fight thoughts, but to let them drift past like half-noticed clouds in a summer sky.**

If students did not experience their anticipated benefits, encourage them to try it again at home or with a friend.

3. Discuss cultural norms

When students don't feel the benefits of meditation, it's not all that surprising. Have students reflect now on how we are taught to "relax" in this culture. Ask students what kinds of messages they get about relaxation. Ask:

■ Is it "okay" to sit alone in a quiet room, not watching television or reading a book, not doing particularly "anything?" Why or why not? How does it feel to do that?

■ It is okay to go for a walk, without a destination or goal in mind?

■ What do you or your family do for vacations? How much actual time is spent "centering" or in "focused rest?" What is the most relaxing part of the vacation?

- What does our cultural "work ethic" have to say about inactive, or "nonproductive" people?

- Are Americans prone to medicating themselves with various drugs (e.g., sedatives, alcohol, muscle relaxers) to calm down? Why do you think they are, or aren't?

- If there are Asian or Indian students in the group, ask them to describe what their parents or culture have taught them about relaxation.

Summarize the session by reviewing the benefits of relaxation. As suggested in *Fighting Invisible Tigers*, relaxation skills are important because they:

1. Help people feel less crazy, worried, and insecure

2. Help people get control of their minds and bodies—a big and important step in and of itself

3. Give the body a chance to recover from the stress of everyday life

4. Can provide enormous amounts of new energy, both physical and mental; can revitalize a person

5. Help people feel good about themselves and about life

4. Collect and assign homework

Collect inventories on physical activity and assign students pages 67-76 in *Fighting Invisible Tigers*. Also, assign them the student inventory on relaxation. Additionally, remind students to begin thinking about the final assignment in which they make a relaxation tape for themselves. Hand out the instruction sheet, go over the assignment, and answer any questions.

Alternative Suggestions

It may help to have some slides or visuals of different relaxation postures and activities. Perhaps posters of different yoga classes or yogis from India; or slides of Buddhist monks in temple, meditating. You may also wish to show video tapes of how relaxation exercises are performed. Local hospitals may have teaching tapes that demonstrate deep breathing techniques for women in childbirth classes. Also, a regional chapter of CEA (Childbirth Education Association) may have tapes to lend. In addition, check with a medical school library if one is nearby; it might have a videotape that demonstrates how progressive relaxation techniques or biofeedback are used in physical therapy. Visuals are particularly helpful in this session, both to create a mood and give students a picture of the activities they're practicing.

References

[1]Samuels, M. and Samuels, N. *Seeing with the Mind's Eye*. New York City: Random House and Bookworks, 1975, p. 106.

[2]Restak, R. *The Brain*. New York City: Bantam Books, 1984.

[3]Ibid

Final Project Instruction Sheet

RELAXATION TAPE

This project is an opportunity for you to:

1. Demonstrate your knowledge about the purposes and procedures of progressive relaxation

2. Build yourself a tailor-made relaxation tool

3. Explore dramatic possibilities in scriptwriting, recording, reading, music selection

You now know something about how progressive relaxation works, having experienced it several times in class. There are a variety of relaxation tapes out on the market, and some of them may work for you. I think it's intriguing, however, to make your own tape. After all, we're all individuals with somewhat different tastes, and may respond differently to different messages, voices, or sequences of relaxing. It's important for you to make a tape that say what YOU want it to say, and is read by you—or someone who gives you confidence, or has a particularly soothing voice. The assignment, therefore, is to make your own audio tape by following the principles of progressive relaxation as we've experienced them, but personalizing it for your needs.

Here are some examples of how tapes may be creatively produced:

■ Ask a favorite or trusted person to record your script.

■ Write special messages into the script, such as reminding yourself to visualize a favorite place or season.

■ When writing the script, choose your own metaphors and similies (e.g., "as calm as the lake on a still summer day;" a "wave of peace washing over me.")

■ Select a soft, relaxing piece of music to accompany the words. Make sure the volume is really low, and the piece doesn't interfere with the reading.

■ Insert an inspiring poem or favorite saying.

■ If you know that much of your tension centers in one part of your body (like your stomach, neck, or jaw), then emphasize that body part in the script.

■ Experiment with different sequences of relaxation. Some people start at the top of their heads and work down, others prefer beginning with the feet and working up.

Tapes should be at least five to ten minutes long. A good way to make a tape is to record the script while a friend actually goes through the relaxation exercise. That will help you adjust the timing and pace of the exercise. If you'd like to read further about relaxation, see me for some suggested books.

The criteria on which I'll be evaluating your tape are:

1. A personalized touch to your script

2. Understanding of progressive relaxation concepts (e.g., techniques such as repetition, calm pace, pauses, positive mood)

3. Care with production (e.g., tape should be audible, at least five minutes long)

4. Extra bonus points for creativity or unusual care with production of tape

STUDENT INVENTORY ON RELAXATION

1. Have you ever been deeply, totally, completely relaxed? (Exclude sleeping.) If so, what did it feel like to be this relaxed?

2. How does this feeling of relaxation compare to the feeling of stress? Compare how your body feels when it's relaxed vs. stressed; compare what your thinking is like; compare what your speech, your relationships with other people are like.

3. Think back over the last twenty-four hours as you did when writing your first inventory on stress. Recall the periods of stress, and the periods of relaxation. Concentrate now on the intervals in which you felt most relaxed. Typically what—or who—helps you to relax? When during an average day do you feel more relaxed?

4. How do you schedule relaxation times into your day? Do you routinely allow yourself some time to restore yourself? Why or why not?

5. How would you describe your average level of anxiety on a scale of 1 - 10? (1 = worried, scattered, strung-out; 10 = calm, relaxed, full of energy.) On the average, how much energy do you have? How able are you to concentrate?

6. What value do you see to regular relaxation?

We all need time to recharge our batteries and release tension. This inventory is a way to see how often we provide that time for ourselves. Feeling extremely anxious, scattered, or lethargic are possible signs of too much unrelieved tension.

Session 6

COMMUNICATION STYLES

Overview

The biggest source of stress for many students lies in the whole area of interpersonal relationships. Teenagers spend a lot of time and emotional energy worrying about their friendships and their relations with parents, siblings, and teachers. Simply communicating their own needs, thoughts, and opinions (both positive and negative) can be stressful. While physical activity and relaxation lifeskills can release tension, assertiveness skills get closer to the problem by mediating stress at its source.

In this session students start to look at the effects of communication styles on relationships. They define assertiveness and learn about passive, aggressive, passive-aggressive, and assertive communication styles.

Learner Outcomes

The purpose of this session is to enable students to:

1. Define passive, aggressive, passive-aggressive, and assertive styles of communication

2. Explain the needs and motivations behind each type of response style, as well as the consequences of each style

3. Identify the benefits of being assertive

4. Identify some of the cultural norms and stereotypes surrounding these behaviors

Agenda

In order to accomplish these outcomes, teachers need to:

1. Describe passive, aggressive, passive-aggressive, and assertive behavior styles (15 min.)

2. Conduct a small group exercise in which students identify and discuss these behaviors in written scenarios (20 min.)

3. Summarize discussion by listing the benefits of assertiveness and the cultural norms that surround each communication style (15 min.)

4. Collect student inventories on relaxation and assign homework

Resources and Materials

1. Blackboard or easel pad

2. Response Style Worksheet (see pages 84-85)

3. Student Inventory on Assertiveness (see page 86)

Activities

1. Describe four response styles

Begin by explaining that assertiveness can be considered one of the most important of all lifeskills because it does something directly about the source of interpersonal stress. Communication styles can either build or prevent stress. Assertiveness is one style of communication that can help people feel less like victims and more in control of their lives. Assertiveness enables a person to protect his or her basic rights while respecting the rights of others. An assertive interpersonal style also leads to more honest, enjoyable, and long-lasting relationships.

Concepts of assertiveness can be traced back to psychologists working in the 1940s, but assertiveness skills weren't systematically defined or taught until the 1970s when assertiveness training became popular. Ask if students can define assertiveness. We favor a definition supplied in *Your Perfect Right*, by Robert Alberti and Michael Emmons:[1]

> Assertive behavior enables a person to act in his or her own best interest, to stand up for herself or himself without undue anxiety, to express honest feelings comfortably, or to exercise personal rights without denying the rights of others. (p. 13)

Ask students to give examples of situations in which people "act in their own best interest," "stand up for themselves," "express their feelings honestly," and "exercise their personal rights without denying the rights of others." Don't rush through this definition as it's important that everyone understand just what kinds of behavior are implied. Of the many examples that could be cited, here are a few:

1. Acting in one's own best interest

- talking to a teacher when confused

- when home with a cold, asking a friend for the homework assignment

- training hard before a team try-out or marathon

- deciding to join, or *not* to join the yearbook staff

- deciding to organize a party or school event

2. Standing up for oneself

- saying "no" to uncomfortable social invitations (e.g., drinking beer, a party, or a ride with unknown kids in a car)

- defending a personal decision, action, or belief

- responding to criticism

- explaining an answer to a (teacher's) question more thoroughly

3. Expressing feelings

- honestly and respectfully disagreeing with a friend

- thanking a parent or sibling for his or her help

- telling someone you're afraid, worried, or angry

- saying "You're great!" or "I like you!"

4. Exercising personal rights

- expressing a political viewpoint

- confronting a teacher, parent, or coach about a problem

- returning defective merchandise

- asking other people not to smoke in a no-smoking area

- asking for feedback or explanations from others

5. Not denying the rights of others

- not calling other people names

- not threatening, bribing, or manipulating other people

- not hurting other people (physically, emotionally)

- not lying about people or events in order to gain control

- respecting each person's independent viewpoint, decisions, needs

Next, define passive, aggressive, and passive-aggressive response styles.

Passive Response

A person operating with a passive response style allows other people to make all the decisions, to control his or her feelings or actions. Overly passive people may not even be aware of having strong feelings or opinions. Because they don't believe their thoughts or feelings "count," they deny their own needs or consistently put them last, and work very hard to please other people. This often leaves passive people feeling hurt, anxious, angry, letdown, and depressed because they can't get their own needs met.

Aggressive Response

In contrast, a person operating with an aggressive response style is apt to be loud, abusive, "pushy," and sarcastic. Examples of an aggressive style include people who: gossip maliciously; boss, tease, or humiliate other people in public; physically threaten others; need to win every argument; or control other people's decisions or feelings. Achieving a personal goal at the expense of others is not a problem for the aggressive person; by definition, his or her own needs come first. While an aggressive style makes people feel powerful on the surface, it costs them a lot in terms of trust and respect. It, too, leaves the person with few close friends and many unmet needs.

Passive-Aggressive Response

People who operate with a passive-aggressive response style combine elements of the two styles above. They do not overtly dominate or abuse other people, but seek control or revenge covertly (sometimes unconsciously) instead. Passive-aggressive people, for example, say "yes" with an insincere smile and never follow through. They are persistently late; their commitments aren't "solid." They keep quiet when an unfair or difficult decision is being made, then quietly sabotage it behind the scenes. Although passive-aggressive people are angry, they don't know how to directly express their anger, and they fear the anger or disapproval of the authorities "in charge." Like passive people, they see themselves as victims who can't change oppressive (or even benign) circumstances. Like aggressive people, their methods for gaining power disrespect the rights and feelings of others.

Explain to students that we all have used passive, aggressive, and passive-aggressive styles of communication at different times in our lives. We're human beings, we're imperfect, so at times we do fail to speak up, or we speak out in anger in an abusive way, or we quietly seek revenge. One hopes we use some assertive behaviors as well. Make sure it's clear that the examples above illustrate people who consistently operate out of one mode and are exaggerations of how most people interact.

When going over these definitions, bring students into the discussion by asking them to provide examples of different response styles, and to compare them.

2. Conduct small group exercise	Have students form small groups and pass around the Response Style Worksheet. For each of the vignettes, have students identify the four different communication styles and to think about the motivations of each of the characters in the scene. Tell them to discuss the imagined consequences of each behavior style. Then ask students to figure out how the situations could be handled differently by an assertive person.
3. Summarize the sessions by listing reasons and norms	To summarize the small group activity (and the session), ask students why they think people—such as the characters in the scenarios—use aggressive, passive-aggressive, and passive response styles. List these reasons on the board and elaborate on them with the motivations provided in the student test (see below):

Why are people passive? *Because ...*

- they don't know how to be assertive
- they fear the loss of approval and support from others
- they want to avoid conflict and keep the peace
- feeling like a victim is all they know
- they mistake assertiveness for aggressiveness
- they mistake passivity for femininity
- they are uncertain about their basic rights
- they get a lot of rewards for being passive
- they fear responsibility, accountability

81

Why are people aggressive? *Because . . .*

- they don't know how to be assertive
- they fear appearing weak or losing control of the situation
- they need to dominate, win, get their way all the time
- they don't know how to compromise, share, or support others
- they mistake aggressiveness for assertiveness
- they mistake aggressiveness for "machismo"
- they're rewarded for being aggressive
- they don't know how to be responsible for and responsive to other people

Why are people passive-aggressive? *Because . . .*

- they don't know how to be assertive
- they are angry but feel guilty about being angry
- they've been punished for expressing their feelings openly
- they're not sure their opinions, feelings, needs "count" as much as other people's
- they resent people in power but are afraid of having power (responsibility) themselves
- they also mistake aggressiveness for assertiveness, and they can't allow themselves to act aggressively

Have students summarize the "consequences" of each response style. Ask, "What happens to the person who is consistently aggressive? How do other kids feel towards her or him?" "What happens to the person who is consistently passive-aggressive? Are his or her goals ever really achieved?" The real "problem" with these response styles is not that they (or the person) are inherently evil, but that they make it practically impossible to have friends or an honest relationship with anyone. They leave all parties concerned frustrated, angry, and lonely. They prolong or create conflict and stress.

Then ask students to think about the "messages" they get from society—their friends, neighbors, families, the media—about assertive, aggressive, and passive response styles. Ask, "How do television characters 'tell' us to act? Who are 'the good guys?'" "It is 'good' to be aggressive? Are men supposed to be aggressive and women passive?"

"Is aggressiveness confused with assertiveness?" Explain that the role models around us may be giving us a simplistic, and misleading, view of relationships.

List the benefits of assertiveness. An assertive style of communication can lead to some awkwardness, particularly at first, and even change some friendships. Over time, however, assertiveness leads to:

- greater self-confidence and self-respect

- the potential for equality among friends, peers, family members

- better friendships, and more supportive friends

- a sense of control (sanity) over "crazy," difficult situations

- a sense that objectives and goals can be reached

- a sense of belonging to a group without sacrificing personal opinions of beliefs

- a sense of responsibility for self and others

- less free-floating anxiety

You'll want to clarify that being assertive doesn't automatically solve every problem, change the world, or enable one to win every battle. Being assertive in an abusive situation, for example, doesn't guarantee that the other person won't continue to act irresponsibly. But it does increase the likelihood that conflicts will decrease. And it helps prevent the feelings of helplessness and anger from becoming overwhelming.

4. Collect inventories on relaxation and assign homework

Have students complete their inventories on assertiveness for next time.

References

[1]Alberti, R.E. and Emmons, M.L. *Your Perfect Right*. San Luis Obispo (Cal.): Impact Publishers, 1982.

RESPONSE STYLE WORKSHEET

For each of the vignettes below, identify which response styles are illustrated. Discuss why the behaviors might be classified as aggressive, assertive, passive, or passive-aggressive. What motivates each character to use their chosen response style? What do you suppose will happen in each scenario?

... two acquaintances, a boy and a girl, meet by accident at a restaurant next to school and decide to have a malt. When the bill comes, the girl stands up to leave without paying. The boy clears his throat and says, "Diane, I probably should have let you know earlier, but I didn't expect to run in to you today, and this has to be Dutch treat today. I'm short of cash."

... older sister has been promising younger sister to return a new sweater she borrowed. The younger sibling has asked for the sweater repeatedly, only to be told "Don't get uptight, it's coming." It's been over four weeks since the sweater was loaned.

... two friends are competing for the position of yearbook editor. Each wants the job, and they are equally qualified. On election day, they have ten minutes to present a final speech to the voters. One candidate announces she is "much more experienced" than her competitor, who "couldn't design a yearbook or write copy to save his life." The other candidate says he'll do his best "to use his two years of experience as assistant editor to serve the wishes of the yearbook committee and the school."

... several teens are eating lunch in a crowded restaurant. Two are smoking, even though they are in the no-smoking section. The waitress asks them to move to the smoking section. One teen gets up rudely and says loudly "No one tells me to move. You don't want me, you don't want my business" and leaves. The other teen sulks, stubs her cigarette out on the counter, and spends the next five minutes slowly packing up her belongings.

... four teenagers are cruising around in one of their parent's car, drinking beer. Two of the kids start to feel uncomfortable with the amount of drinking going on. Every time the subject of going home comes up, the teen who's driving says "You're a bunch of babies! This is our chance to have fun!" The group stays out until 1:30 a.m., when the driver decides to go home.

... two girls are at a shopping mall buying some blouses. At the checkout counter, one notices two missing buttons on the blouse she's selected and asks if she can exchange it for another. "That's the last one, honey," she's told. She leaves with the blouse, paying full price.

... a small group of students are discussing the town mayor and his reelection campaign. Three of the four students are arguing vociferously: "You dolt! Only an idiot believes this guy is for real!" "You Democrats are all alike." "What's this guy's voting record, if you're so smart?" The fourth student is silent.

... on their way to a basketball game, two girls are offered a ride by some boys they've seen around school but don't know. They decline by saying, "Thanks a lot, but we'd rather walk just now. Maybe we'll see you there."

... son is not looking forward to another year of school. So much of it is boring. His father expects so much of him scholastically, and has him signed up for all the advanced math courses in the school. He used to like math, but not this much. Son starts the school year thinking maybe it will be better, and his father won't make him study so hard.

... a teacher finishes describing an assignment and dismisses the class. As the class files out, one student approaches the teacher saying, "I'm interested in the topic you've assigned, but I thought you should know I wrote a similar paper last quarter. May I choose a related topic?" Meanwhile, another student in the back of the room slams down her books, throws the teacher a disgusted look, and leaves the room muttering, "If she thinks I'm going to write another paper on that stupid subject, she's dumber than she looks."

STUDENT INVENTORY ON ASSERTIVENESS

1. It's an imperfect world. Justice does not always prevail. Life is not always fair. The concept of innate, human rights is one of the most important and marvelous constructs of a modern democratic society; without a sense of basic rights, people cannot live together without destroying each other. Can you identify any basic human rights which you feel should be universally protected, which you would ideally wish to protect for yourself and others?

2. Describe someone who acts assertively.

3. Describe someone who acts aggressively.

4. Describe someone who acts passively.

5. Describe someone who acts passive-aggressively.

6. Some of us respond aggressively when we feel "attacked" . . . by tigers, or other stress triggers; others retreat. What do you know about your own response styles—your own predisposition to act assertively, passively, etc., when challenged?

7. Describe any benefits you've experienced from responding assertively in situations.

8. Describe any drawbacks you've experienced when responding with passive, aggressive, or passive-aggressive response styles.

Learning more about yourself and your response styles is critical for getting along with people, whether they are friends, parents, co-workers, siblings, or "enemies." It takes a lot of patience and thought to identify human rights and learn the positive skills of assertiveness that will protect these rights for you and others. Use the thoughts you've gathered here to become more conscious of your response styles.

Session 7

BEING ASSERTIVE

Overview

To start thinking and acting more assertively, it's important to articulate and reaffirm the basic human rights to which we're all entitled. Knowledge of these rights gives us courage to defend them, and reminds us to respect them in others. In the first part of this session, students draw up their own "Bill of Rights."

Role playing assertiveness is a good way to practice and feel comfortable using these skills. In the second half of this session, the A.S.S.E.R.T. formula is used to help students think through assertive responses in role plays that dramatize conflicts and the violation of rights.

Learner Outcomes

The purpose of this session is to enable students to:

1. Identify basic human rights they wish to respect

2. Identify steps in responding assertively

3. Practice being assertive

Agenda

In order to accomplish these outcomes, teachers need to:

1. Lead a class discussion and construct a "Class Bill of Rights" (15 min.)

2. Explain the A.S.S.E.R.T. Formula (10 min.)

3. Monitor small group role plays in which students apply the formula (25 min.)

4. Collect inventories on assertiveness and assign homework

Resources and Materials

1. The A.S.S.E.R.T. Formula (see pages 91)

2. Assertiveness Role Plays (see pages 92-94)

3. Blackboard or easel pad

Activities

1. Class discussion on basic rights

Quickly review some of the main points on assertiveness skills from the previous session, such as: (a) their importance to human relationships, and (b) the basic differences between passive, aggressive, passive-aggressive, and assertive response styles. Explain that it's difficult to be assertive if you don't know what rights you've entitled to, or don't believe these rights apply to you.

Ask students to name some general rights to which they believe all human beings should be entitled. What are they? Ask them, if they were to construct their own Bill of Rights as a group, what would be in it? (You also may want to refer to page 73 in **_Fighting Invisible Tigers: A Stress Management Guide For Teens_**) This Bill of Rights should reflect the context of students' lives and their needs and feelings more than the rights of nations or citizens. Thus, instead of "right to bear arms," they may wish to list "right to having a voice in certain school rules and regulations," or "right to honest answers from friends and teachers," or "right to say no."

List these rights on a tablet or blackboard. It's not important for students to vote on the list or come to consensus on the priority of its items. Do encourage some discussion of the items and explore why (or why not) the suggested rights should be respected. If necessary, clarify the difference between "right" and "privilege." (It's our right as citizens in a democratic society to vote; it's a privilege to drive a Cadillac.) If students wish to have a right listed, ask them how they could protect this right without abusing other people's rights. Ask them whether their suggestions are attainable, and whether they are prepared to entitle other people to this right as well.

2. The A.S.S.E.R.T. Formula

Pass around the student handout with the A.S.S.E.R.T. Formula. Explain that the formula is useful for learning how to think through an assertive response. When rights or feeling have been abused, people typically respond reflexively with whatever response mode they've adopted. They either attack, withdraw, or think of a way to get even. The "attack" and "withdraw" behaviors are none other than our passive and aggressive response styles. The A.S.S.E.R.T. Formula

88

interrupts the habitual response with a set of suggestions for thinking about and constructing a better response.

As with any new skill, the A.S.S.E.R.T. Formula feels cumbersome in the beginning, but with time it feels more natural. Explain that each letter in the acronym stands for a suggested step in framing an assertive response. These steps should be taken in a sequence.

- **"A" stands for "attention."** Before you can solve your problem, you first have to get the other person to agree to listen to you. Find a time, or place, or method which helps them focus their attention on you.

- The first **"S" stands for "soon, simple, and short."** When possible, speak up as soon as you realize your rights have been violated. ("Soon" may be a matter of seconds, hours, or days.) Look the person in the eye and keep your comments to the point.

- The second **"S" stands for "specific behavior."** Focus on the behavior the person used that compromised your rights, not the person himself or herself, or else he or she will feel "attacked." Tell the person exactly which behavior disturbed you.

- **"E" stands for "effect on me."** Share the feelings you experienced as as result of this person's behavior, such as: "I get angry when . . . " or "I get frustrated when . . . "

- **"R" stands for "response."** Describe your preferred outcome, what you'd like to see happen instead, and ask for some feedback on it.

- **"T" stands for "terms."** If all goes well, you may be able to make an agreement with the other person about how to handle the situation in the future. Or, you may "agree to disagree (respectfully)," or simply come to an impasse. Even if no agreement has been reached, you've accomplished your first goal, which is to assert yourself with dignity.

Generally speaking, its important to respond as soon as possible to a violation of rights, but it's not always possible to do that. First of all, it may take time to recognize that one's rights have been violated. People don't always realize that their feelings have been hurt. Second, it's not easy to think clearly when issues are emotionally charged. Third, it may be better to wait for a time when the other person is more receptive to talking with you. Sometimes it's appropriate to follow up a conflict with a letter, phone call, or conference. Sometimes the only way people can logistically make amends is later in time. Students should not feel bad if they miss their first opportunity to assert themselves. Communicating needs assertively, even when it's done weeks later, can raise self-esteem and improve a relationship.

Answer any questions students have about the formula and explain that they'll be practicing it in the next exercise.

3. Monitor small group role plays	Have students form small groups of three to five people. Pass around the handout, "Assertiveness Role Plays," and tell students to assign themselves the different roles. Each student should have the opportunity to practice the A.S.S.E.R.T. formula at least once. To help the exercise get off the ground, circulate among the groups and answer questions, help settle role assignments, or rephrase the purpose of the activity. Encourage students to be dramatic, to exaggerate the particular communication mode that's involved.
	At the end of class, summarize the activity by asking students to report on their experiences. Ask: "How did it feel to be standing up for your rights? How did it feel to ask for help?" and other similar questions.
4. Collect inventories on assertiveness and assign homework	For the next time, students should read pages 77-86 in ***Fighting Invisible Tigers***.

THE A.S.S.E.R.T. FORMULA

"A" stands for "attention."

Before you can solve your problem, you first have to get the other person to agree to listen to you. Find a time, or place, or method which helps them focus their attention on you.

The first "S" stands for "soon, simple, and short."

When possible, speak up as soon as you realize your rights have been violated. ("Soon" may be a matter of seconds, hours, or days.) Look the person in the eye and keep your comments to the point.

The second "S" stands for "specific behavior."

Focus on the behavior the person used that compromised your rights, not the person himself or herself, or else he or she will feel "attacked." Tell the person exactly which behavior disturbed you.

"E" stands for "effect on me."

Share the feelings you experienced as as result of this person's behavior, such as: "I get angry when . . . " or "I get frustrated when . . . "

"R" stands for "response."

Describe your preferred outcome, what you'd like to see happen instead, and ask for some feedback on it.

"T" stands for "terms."

If all goes well, you may be able to make an agreement with the other person about how to handle the situation in the future. Or, you may "agree to disagree (respectfully)," or simply come to an impasse.

EVEN IF NO AGREEMENT HAS BEEN REACHED, YOU'VE ACCOMPLISHED YOUR GOAL OF ASSERTING YOURSELF WITH DIGNITY.

ASSERTIVENESS ROLE PLAYS

Scenario A

A guy is pressing a female acquaintance for information concerning her best friend's "romances." He wants to know everything about this friend—who she's dating, how often she is seeing a particular person, etc.

Characters: The Guy

The Girl Being Questioned

Guy: Your job is to badger the girl until she tells you what you want to know, or until she makes it clear that she will not reveal any more information. Secretly, you'd like to date this girl's friend, but you also enjoy a bit of teasing and the chance to spread a good rumor. You're a fast talker; be cagey, be aggressive, be "hard to say no to."

Girl: Your job is to decide how you want to handle this. You don't know this guy well, aren't sure you trust him, yet heard your friend say she thought he was cute. You want to protect your friend's privacy and are not sure how to get this guy to leave you alone.

Role play the scenes as people in improvisational drama do: think through your character for a few moments, make up a few lines of dialogue that this character would be likely to say, and make up the scene as you go.

After letting the scene unfold for a couple of moments, stop the action. Ask students viewing the drama to brainstorm suggestions for the characters; see how using the A.S.S.E.R.T. formula would help the characters in the drama. Redo the role play using the new suggestions.

● ●

Scenario B

A mother is getting increasingly concerned about the way her teenage daughter has been dressing. Particularly aggravating to her are the punk clothes and spiked hairstyle. Recently, the daughter's been leaving the house wearing only a jean jacket, although it's the dead of winter. One Saturday evening the parents are entertaining a group of neighbors. The daughter sneaks down the stairs, hoping for a quick exit. Too late! Mother shrieks right in front of the guests about her thin jacket.

Characters: Mother

Daughter

Guests (2 or 3)

Mother: Your job is to convey total exasperation and frustration. You've talked with your daughter so many times about her manner of dress, her hairstyle, at least she could wear enough warm clothing. This time she's humiliated you in front of your friends, who were just discussing the importance of teenagers respecting adults. You want her to wear a jacket, but you don't want (your daughter) to create a scene.

Daughter: Your job is to assert yourself without making things worse; your mother is likely to ground you. Plus, you're dating a son of one of the couples at the table, and don't want to appear completely ridiculous. At the same time, if you have to put on the sweater your mother likes, you'll die of embarrassment. How will you convince her you're old enough to make these kinds of decisions for yourself?

Guests: Your job is to decide whether to interject anything in the conversation or not. The scene is getting awkward. Should you ignore it, help the mother, or help the daughter?

As with the first role play, prepare your character, then let the action roll. After the scene reaches some sort of conclusion, stop the action. Other students watching the role play can comment on who was behaving aggressively, assertively, etc., and suggest ways the **A.S.S.E.R.T.** formula may help restructure some of the responses. Redo the role play with the new responses.

● ●

Scenario C

Two friends are walking to class. One friend asks the other for a textbook that was loaned to him several weeks ago. The owner of the book needs it now to study for the geology exam. The friend has unfortunately misplaced the book, and doesn't know where it is, but is afraid to say so because the book cost quite a bit and he can't afford to replace it.

Characters: Owner of the textbook

Borrower of the textbook

Owner: Your job is to become increasingly worried about where your textbook is. At first you wanted to simply remind your friend that you need it by the end of the day. When he answers you vaguely, you begin to get angry. If you don't get that book back, you'll have a very difficult time studying for the exam. (You could have asked for it back several weeks ago, but waited until the last minute to study.) Be persistent.

Borrower: Your job is to get pretty anxious about confessing the temporary "loss" of the book. Your friend has a terrible temper. You didn't mean to lose it—you don't think you did, at any rate. It somehow disappeared after the time he left you in the library to walk a girlfriend home. Be vague, inconsistent, and eager to get this guy off your back. You have your own troubles with the geology exam.

As with the other role plays, develop your character for a few moments then launch into action. Use the group to sort through the possible ways for both parties to assert themselves fairly. Who is acting aggressively, who is acting passive-aggressively? Redo the scenario with some revised dialogue.

● ●

Session 8

FRIENDSHIP LEVELS

Overview

Friendships are wonderful buffers to stress, as this and the following session on supportive relationships illustrate. Most people find that it's helpful to have a range of friends, a variety of relationships that not only fulfill different needs but achieve different levels of closeness. "Intimacy levels" can be arranged on a continuum ranging from Level 1 (superficial or brief acquaintances) to Level 5 (enduring, close relationships). Students consider the ways in which people communicate at each level of intimacy and practice different levels of dialogue with a partner. Group identity is also reinforced in this session with a closing appreciation exercise.

Learner Outcomes

The purpose of this session is to enable students to:

1. Define levels of intimacy in relationships

2. Identify the characteristics of language used at each level

3. Practice communicating at three or four of the five levels

4. Practice giving and receiving group support

Agenda

In order to accomplish these outcomes, teachers need to:

1. Lead a group discussion on intimacy levels (20 min.)

2. Supervise an exercise in which partners practice communicating at different levels (20 min.)

3. Conduct a Wonderful Circle (10 min.)

4. Collect and assign homework

Resources and Materials

1. Levels of Intimacy (see pages 100-101)

2. Student Inventory on Relationships (see page 102)

Activities

1. Discussion on intimacy

Intimacy is a scary word. For many people, intimacy is a scary proposition! What does it mean? Some people mistakenly equate it with sexual closeness—which is only one of its many forms. The dictionary defines intimacy as "closely associated." What are some examples of closely related people? Prisoners in a jail cell? Survivors of an airplane crash? Campers on a two-week trek into the wilderness? There are actually many levels of closeness—and quite a range of relationships, from fairly distant to very intimate. Having this range of friendships is healthy; it provides us with a buffer against stress.

Tell students you're going to be discussing levels of closeness and ask them to think about all the people that they know, and how well they know them. Chances are, they've known a lot of people superficially, but only a few really well. In the first part of the discussion, get students to recognize that a range of friends, and a range in the degree of closeness of relationships, is a good thing. Get them thinking by asking questions such as:

- Have you ever lived with someone for a long time yet wondered if you *really* knew them? How can that be?

- Have you ever found yourself surprised by a friend or relative—surprised by something they've said or done that seemed totally out of character—and wondered what they're "really like?" Why aren't people always the same?

- Have you ever sat next to a stranger but within a short amount of time felt you already "knew" him or her, or could become close friends very soon? Why do you suppose that is?

- Are you likely to tell some things to one friend or parent, and other things to another? Why is that?

- How much do you want people in your class or school (generally) to know about you? Why?

■ Are there some things you don't wish to share
  with anyone? Why?

■ If you were on a deserted island, how many people would you
  want with you, and why?

Questions such as these lead to the general point that people often
disclose different amounts of themselves at different times to different
people. We often need to preserve our more private feelings for the few
people we really trust. Those people are very special to us. Other
people we may have fun with, enjoy doing things with, but choose not
to share much of ourselves with—perhaps because circumstances
dictate a certain formality, or because we lack mutual interests,
time, or energy.

At this point ask students to recall from their reading how many levels
of intimacy can be defined, and what types of communication
characterize each level. Ask for examples of statements at each level.
As listed in *Fighting Invisible Tigers: A Stress Management Guide
For Teens:*

■ *Level 1* relationships deal with facts—safe, nonthreatening
  objective information about activities or events in common
  (like the weather or homework assignments).

■ *Level 2* relationships pass around or discuss other people's
  opinions (but not your own). This is "they say" territory, which
  makes it pretty safe.

■ *Level 3* relationships enter "I think" land. Here you offer
  subjective opinions about fact. The other person gets to know
  you from an intellectual perspective. This involves some risk-
  taking because you open yourself up to possible conflict and
  rejection.

■ *Level 4* relationships venture into feelings. You express feelings
  to and experience feelings *with* a listener. (If communicating
  on the same level, the listener will also experience those
  feelings.) Since it's far more risky to share from your heart
  than your head, you become vulnerable and require more trust
  in your relationship with the listener. If trust exists you can
  feel genuinely connected with the other person.

■ *Level 5* relationships are those in which you can share your
  feelings about the other person and your relationship here and

now. They can't be forced or play-acted; they grow out of Level 4 friendships. They involve the most disclosure, the greatest risk, the deepest sharing, the highest degree of trust, and the most intense emotions.

Ask students to mentally categorize where their friends and family members would fit—in which level of intimacy. Reconfirm that it's impossible, and undesirable, to turn every friend into a Level 5. We need the 1's and 2's in our life,too. Ultimately, however, we need to develop the capacity to operate at Levels 4 or 5 ourselves, and to seek out other people who will perform as 4's and 5's to us.

2. Conduct partnership activity

Distribute the Levels of Intimacy handout and tell students to link up with one other person in the room who has a birthday in a month other than their own. Then explain that in the next exercise they're going to practice communicating messages at different levels of intimacy, beginning with Level 1 and working up to either Level 4 or 5. First they should choose a topic (any topic): sports, families, school, movies. Then walk the students through the exercise taking a few minutes at each level of intimacy. After exchanging statements at each level, students should discuss how it *feels* to communicate at various levels. After each two-to-three minute discussion ask, "How did it feel having this type of conversation?"

3. Wonderful circle

After summarizing the partnership activity, bring students together for a closing group exercise.

*Script for Wonderful Circle**

Nothing sows the seeds for a good, lasting relationship as well as remembering to tell people we care about them and that they are wonderful. Every person does have some wonderful aspect. We need to remember to think about all the positive things about our friends and family (and ourselves) and to share our appreciation with them.

When was the last time your best friend told you how wonderful he or she thinks you are? For some reason, the older we get, the less we get to hear from other people about what we're doing well. So let's take

*From *Playfair: Everybody's Guide to Noncompetitive Play* © by Matt Weinstein and Joel Goodman. Reproduced for ***Fighting Invisible Tigers: A Stress Management Guide For Teens*** by permission of Impact Publishers, Inc. P.O. Box 1094, San Luis Obispo, CA 93406. Further reproduction prohibited.

some time right now to share with each other what it is we like about this class, this time together. And you know that we've all been trained very well to do the opposite of that— everyone here is probably an expert at saying what it is we don't like about somebody or something. I want you to put that critical side of you aside right now, and concentrate on appreciating the experience you had here today with your partner and classmates.

Let's get into a big circle with our arms around each other's waists . . . . We'll start by taking a few small steps to the left, and we'll keep going to the left until somebody says "Stop!" Then that person will share something she or he felt good about today. You might want to say you felt good about yourself, something you learned or discovered. Or you might want to appreciate a positive interaction you had with another person, or share the good feelings you have about the group as a whole.

When you've finished your brief sharing, say "Go!" and we'll all take a few small steps in the other direction until someone else says "Stop!" and shares something she or he is feeling good about. We'll continue doing this until every one who wishes to say something has had a chance to say it.

4. Collect and assign homework

Assign the Student Inventory on Relationships and pages 87-102 in *Fighting Invisible Tigers*.

Alternative Suggestions

If you wish, finish the class with a "spontaneous" standing ovation for the group as a whole. Should you decide to do this, assign students the homework before the Wonderful Circle.

LEVELS OF INTIMACY

Communication Exercise

Instructions: Find your partner. Choose a topic together. Discuss the topic from the perspective of each level of intimacy. For example:

Level 1
(FACTS):

Tell each other facts and information about your topic.

Level 2
(OTHERS):

Tell each other what "they say" and do about the topic . . . others in general, or someone you know.

Level 3
(THINK):

Tell each other about your ideas on the subject, what you actually think, your opinions.

Level 4
(FEEL):

Share with each other how you feel about the topic. Talk about what you like, dislike, are happy about, discouraged, or angry.

Level 5
(WE ARE):

Share how it feels to discuss this topic with each other, in this moment. Talk about any reservations you've had and what you have enjoyed about being with this person.

If you finish before the time is up, choose another topic (one that may be more difficult) and go through the exercise again.

THE FIVE LEVELS OF INTIMACY

1 .... 2 .... 3 .... 4 5

FACTS **THEY SAY** **I THINK** **I FEEL** **WE ARE**

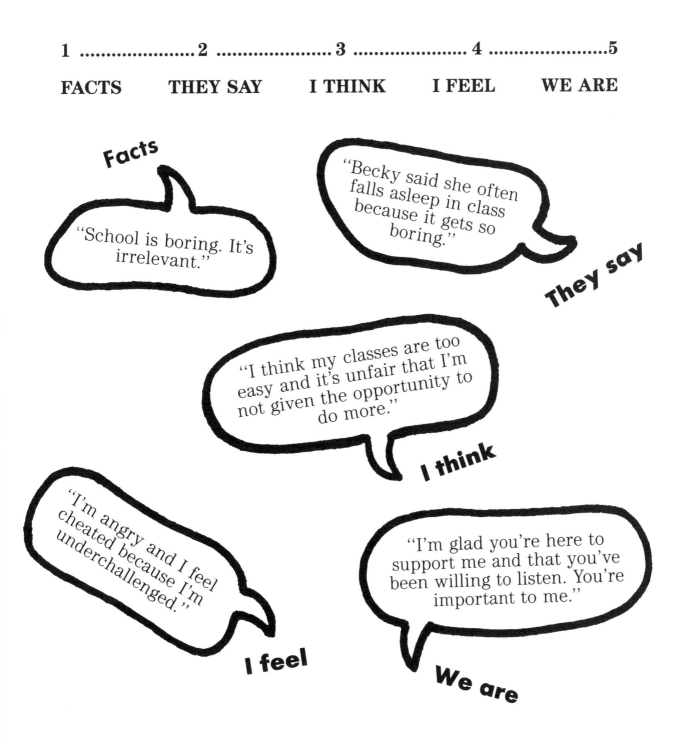

Facts

"School is boring. It's irrelevant."

"Becky said she often falls asleep in class because it gets so boring."

They say

"I think my classes are too easy and it's unfair that I'm not given the opportunity to do more."

I think

"I'm angry and I feel cheated because I'm underchallenged."

I feel

"I'm glad you're here to support me and that you've been willing to listen. You're important to me."

We are

101

STUDENT INVENTORY ON RELATIONSHIPS

1. Why do people need other people?

2. Describe what relationships are like at stages 1, 2, 3, 4, and 5. If you can, think of real people in your life, and describe how you and they relate.

3. How does it feel to use communication skills such as (a) stating feelings, (b) listening, (c) responding with an uncritical attitude, and (d) offering support? Which of these skills seems most difficult for you to do? Why? Which of these skills would you most like to have your friends or relatives use with you? Why?

4. What are some of the benefits, joys, you've experienced from having a really close friend or family member (i.e., a Level 4 or 5)?

5. What are some of the problems and difficulties involved with having a Level 4 or 5 relationship?

6. How would you describe your readiness to be, or interest in being a Level 4 or 5 friend? Is that degree of intimacy something you want or feel ready for?

7. Learning to identify how close you want to be with people (how much you need or desire intimacy), and then learning the skills to foster that intimacy, are two of the most difficult things in life for teens and adults alike. Intimacy creates stress as well as alleviates it. To be a good stress manager, you'll want to reflect on the levels of friendship that you have and wish to cultivate.

Session 9

WEAVING A SAFETY NET

Overview

Relationships are central to stress management. Supportive family members, friends, and others help us deal with fear, frustration, stress, isolation, and other blocks to personal growth. People need other people in order to celebrate, to mourn, to learn from, and to increase our enjoyment of life. But in order to develop supportive relationships, one has to develop (and apply) the basic communication skills of listening, expressing feelings, responding nonjudgementally, and asking for help.

In this session, supportive relationships are explored and celebrated in a playful group exercise. The issues of risk and trust are explored, and a circle exercise in communication skills is conducted.

Learner Outcomes

The purpose of this session is to enable students to:

1. Articulate the role of risk and trust in developing supporting relationships

2. Recognize the importance of supportive relationships to stress management

3. Verbalize four types of "feeling" messages

4. Identify the cultural norms surrounding relationship skills

Agenda

In order to accomplish these outcomes, teachers need to:

1. Conduct the Moonwalk exercise (15 min.)

103

2. Lead a group discussion on the issues of risk, trust, and the overall importance of supportive relationships (10 min.)

3. Conduct a circle exercise in which students expand their "feelings vocabulary" by practicing four types of communication (20 min.)

4. Summarize the cultural norms surrounding relationship building (5 min.)

5. Assign homework

Resources and Materials

1. Large, open space such as a gym or lunchroom cleared of tables and chairs

Activities

1. Conduct the Moonwalk exercise

Introduce this exercise by talking about the importance of play to friendships. Today you're going to start out with a noncompetitive "game"— there are no winners, losers, or tricks to figure out—but it's a game in the sense of playful exercise. Explain that in good friendships, both (all) partners get a chance to give as well as get; everyone has the opportunity to support others, as well as to receive support. When we have the support of our friends and families, we're able to grow, to take risks, to "jump higher" than we can without them.

Script for Moonwalk*

Join up with two other people who are wearing an article of clothing the same color as something of yours. In this exercise, we're going to simulate what it might be like to take a jump where gravity is weaker than the earth's— like on the moon.

In each trio, one person stands in the middle, with hands firmly on hips. The two partners stand on either side and grab the middle person's wrists and forearms (just below the elbows) gently but firmly. The person in the middle counts down "Three, two, one!" and on

*From *Playfair: Everybody's Guide to Noncompetitive Play* © by Matt Weinstein and Joel Goodman. Reproduced for ***Fighting Invisible Tigers: A Stress Management Guide For Teens*** by permission of Impact Publishers, Inc. P.O. Box 1094, San Luis Obispo, CA 93406. Further reproduction prohibited.

"One!" jumps high into the air. At the same time the two partners lift the jumper gently into the air, giving some extra support to allow a jump which is higher than normal. Just give a bit of an extra lift—don't fling, heave, or toss your jumper into the air. Most important, make sure they land safely. Keep it fun: the person in the middle should control how high he or she wants to go. Start out with small lifts and then go a little higher if it's okay with the person in the middle.

When you're in the middle, keep your hands firmly planted on your hips the whole time. If you keep your hands on your hips, then your partners can really help control your flight and can make sure you have a soft landing. Each of you will get a turn being the person in the middle, and will have three jumps apiece. Make sure your threesome is far enough away from the other groups so that you won't crash-land into anyone else. Decide who's going to take the first moonwalk and blast off!

2. Group discussion on supportive relationships

Ask students to collect themselves, then join you in a circle. Have students describe what it felt like to be hoisted into the air by their classmates. Were they excited? Did they feel elated, silly, tense, or scared? Worried about their safety? Disappointed they couldn't be lifted higher? Appreciative and grateful to be delivered home safely? The experience people often have with the exercise is a small "taste" of what they experience in relationships: some insecurity at having to depend on other people, and some thrill of feeling their support.

Either frame questions around the issues of risk and trust in relationships, or simply talk about these issues and invite students to comment. Trust is the most important characteristic of supportive relationships. It's the ingredient that raises a relationship from a 2 or 3 on the intimacy scale to a 4 or 5. Trust results when people start to take risks with each other: they risk their "real" feelings, and dare to show their "real" selves. For most people, taking these risks involves fear; fear of rejection, fear of feeling foolish, fear of being dependent or reliant on someone else.

Enlarge the discussion by going around the circle and asking each person to say one word or one sentence on why relationships are important. Your objective is to help students recognize why people need other people, and to articulate what friends and supportive adults can do for one another. Some sample orienting questions: "In one sentence, tell me what a supportive network of friends or family means to you." "Do people need other people? Why? When?" "What is homesickness? What is a homesick person missing?" "Why are widowers at greater risk for illness and death than adults whose spouses are alive?" When each person has had an opportunity to answer, summarize their answers (or ask a student to do so) and relate them to the management of stress.

3. Practice four types of communication

Staying in the same group circle, ask students to recall (from the student text) the four communication skill areas that help create and sustain supportive relationships. These skill areas include:

- the ability to express feelings

- the ability to listen openly and noncritically

- the ability to offer positive feedback to others

- the ability to ask for support from others

The abilities are all characteristic of people with supportive relationships. People who tell others how they feel, who listen to friends or acquaintances without rushing to judge them, who support others in need, and can ask for support for themselves are people with strong relationship skills. To master these skills, we may need to enlarge our "feelings vocabulary." Sometimes we want to express ourselves or do the right thing, but the words don't come. We haven't had enough practice verbalizing emotions to be able to identify, convey or act upon them.

To enlarge students' vocabularies and to role-play these skills, continue around the circle, asking students to generate a response (one at a time) to one of the prompts provided below. The prompts are in four categories, matching the four skill areas listed above. Tell them to keep their responses short and simple. You will probably want to give the same prompt to two or three students in order to compare; the range of possible reactions, and "stretch" their vocabularies. Several examples of prompts are listed, but you'll need to develop more if you want each student to have a different prompt.

Prompts for Communication Exercise

Express feelings

How would you feel if . . .

- *a beloved grandparent was sick and likely to die?*

- *a teacher said you were not working up to your potential?*

- *there was a big party and no one invited you?*

■ *your mom and dad had a major fight?*

■ *your younger brother just made Most Valuable Player on the JV hockey team?*

■ *you found out someone was spreading rumors about you?*

Listen openly and noncritically

How would you respond to someone who said . . .

■ *"This class is so bad I'm going to skip out today."*

■ *"I'm going to be a millionaire some day."*

■ *"No one cares about me, and it's just too hard to stick around here."*

■ *"No matter what I do, my life doesn't get any better."*

Offer positive feedback

■ *has been a good friend for the last three years?*

■ *tried out for a part in the school play and didn't make it?*

■ *submitted a poorly written article to the school newspaper (and you are the editor)?*

■ *asks you for your opinion of their new clothes?*

■ *has shown a lot of courage?*

Ask for support

Everyone think for a moment of an upcoming issue for which you need support from other people. Some test, or experience, or decision, that you have looming over you, that might be a little easier to confront if you had support (or signs of support) from others.

■ *What sign(s) of support would make it easier?*

■ *Of whom or from whom would you ask it?*

■ *How would you ask?*

Encourage students to explore their feelings and communication skills with this exercise. Push them to describe their feelings with words other than "sad," "mad," "glad," and "bad." Challenge them to describe conflicting emotions ("I was happy for my brother, in a way, after he made most valuable player—not that he deserved it, but I think it's lousy that I never got it."). See how many different words and phrases students can generate after each prompt. If you're getting monosyllabic replies, keep saying: "Tell me more. What else?"

Similarly, encourage them to consider how they might respond nonverbally in one of the given situations. Listening noncritically involves more nonverbal communication than verbal. How is it done? Offering support to others may be accomplished more effectively with a gesture (i.e., walking someone home from school, sending cards, giving a hug) than a speech.

By making the "partner" in the interaction imaginary (the prompt takes the place of the partner), students are relieved of actual confrontations. They don't have to reveal their "real" feelings to each other, or recall personal experiences. This should, we hope, free them up to imagine lots of responses. Nonetheless, the exercise may also touch on some actual dialogues students have had (or wish to have), and help prepare them for future communications. The last series of prompts (i.e., "asking for support") is a most direct example of this transference.

4. Summarize cultural norms

Close the session by quickly summarizing how our culture does and does not teach the skills of relationship building. Again, the famous American "pioneer spirit" often prevents us from asking for help. We choose to go it alone. The recent "Me Generation" of the 1970s sanctioned the pursuit of personal goals to a great extent. Meanwhile, our Puritan ethic, northern European influence told us to internalize our feelings, and not to speak of our pain. While most of us are experts at criticizing, we're less skilled at recognizing how much we appreciate friendships, or the efforts of others.

5. Collect the Student Inventory on Relationships

Assign students to begin work on their relaxation tape, and to be thinking of which lifeskill area they wish to pursue for their growth contract.

Session 10

SCRIPTING THE FUTURE

Overview

Perhaps the most difficult of all lifeskills to master is that of creating a personal vision for oneself, and then taking responsibility for turning that vision into reality. To do so involves lots of introspective, risk-taking, patience, support, and just plain courage. To become self-directed, people need to know: (1) who they are, (2) what is of value and what they want out of life, and (3) how to negotiate hurdles, and acquire the skills and experience needed to achieve that vision.

This session deals with the first two parts of this process. First, the cultural supports and deterrents to self-directedness are discussed, and second, students engage in a values clarification exercise to explore goals and values. This is followed by a discussion in which students' obstacles and resources are identified.

Although "scripting one's future" does cause anxiety, living someone else's agenda (or worse, living with no agenda at all) is much more stressful, and ultimately, unfulfilling. Fortunately, the previously learned lifeskills of relaxation, physical activity, supportive relationships, and assertiveness are all powerful tools that help with the discomfort.

Learner Outcomes

The purpose of this session is to enable students to:

1. Identify the forces that support and hinder their process of self-awareness/self-discovery

2. Identify some of their enduring interests, needs, values, and goals

3. Identify roadblocks and hurdles they'll need to overcome

4. Identify one immediate step toward pursuing a future goal

109

Agenda

In order to accomplish these outcomes, teachers need to:

1. Lead a group discussion on the forces that support and hinder self-awareness (10 min.)

2. Conduct a value clarification exercise (20 min.)

3. Lead a group discussion on ways to take charge of one's life (15 min.)

4. Assign homework

Resources and Materials

1. Future Scripts (see page 113)

2. Student Inventory on Life Planning Skills (see page 114)

3. Blackboard or easel pad

Activities

1. Identify forces

Introduce the discussion by explaining how this lifeskill, taking charge of your life, involves several steps: creating a personal vision for the future, and planning how to get there. In the next session you're going to concentrate more on the second half of that process—planning how to get there. In this session students are going to look at what they want for the future. Explain that it takes time to become self-directed and responsible for one's future, partly because it takes such a long time to figure out who we are (our enduring interests, needs, abilities) and what we really want in life (values, goals). It takes a while to see which decisions are "the big decisions," and to understand who's been influencing these decisions.

Ask students to think for a moment about the people or "things" (i.e., systems, messages, influences) in our society that make it difficult for us to find out who we are and what we want, or that restrict us in pursuing our goals. Then, ask them to think of the people or "things" in our society that help us *gain* self-awareness and pursue our goals. Possible responses to list on the board are:

People or things that make it difficult for students to gain self-awareness or pursue personal goals . . .

■ Parents who are overly directive, have high expectations in certain areas of achievement or behavior

- Inflexible school systems or curricula that limit options and demand conformity

- Cultural or sexual stereotypes that restrict visions for self

- Powerful cliques at school that dominate taste, behaviors

- Self: fear of failure, desire to please others

People or things that help students gain self-awareness or pursue personal goals . . .

- Supportive parent, relative, teacher, or counselor

- Supportive friends

- Particular courses in school

- Opportunities to try special classes, attend summer events, to travel or have experiences away from home

- Self: through journal writing or other modes of introspection

Help students realize that there are, and always will be, other people whose influence or concerns will affect our life decisions. This doesn't mean that we always have to sit "at the back of the tandem bicycle." We *can* learn to direct our own destiny.

Here is where assertiveness skills pay off; the so-called "Big Decision-makers" (such as parents and teachers) often have less power than kids want to believe. Most are willing to negotiate with students who are willing to assume responsibility and control. In the end, the most important decision-makers (with regard to their own lives) are students themselves. They are, ultimately, the people who determine what to do with themselves, their lives, their options. This doesn't mean that they (or we) have the power to make *all* our dreams come true. But in the end, we are responsible for choosing our dreams, and for learning how to pursue them.

2. **Values Clarification Exercise**

The purpose of this exercise is to give students permission to start dreaming their own dreams, to be idealistic, think beyond the confines of their present lives, and to center in on who they want to be and what they want to accomplish in life. Explain that in this exercise students should put all the obstructions and messages from outside aside for a moment, and allow themselves to script their own future. Have them take out several sheets of paper and give them the following instructions.

111

Script for Values Clarification Exercise

In the next 20 minutes, I want you to imagine you are an accomplished film writer, writing to a studio executive who has contracted to produce your next picture. You've got a great idea for a film and you're going to tell him or her about it. You describe, in the first two or three paragraphs, the plot of the film. In the next couple of paragraphs, you describe as much as you can about the main character. There are only three additional rules for this exercise: first, the main character described in the letter has to be you, as you imagine yourself in the future, in the prime of life. Second, the plot should focus on your future life (after you finish school), although it may reference your past. Third, the outcome of the story should reflect what you would ***most*** like to have happen to you.

If necessary, list on the board the instructions: "two - three paragraphs on plot;" "two - three paragraphs on main character," "what you want to happen."

3. Discuss taking charge of one's life

When students are done, ask for a few volunteers to share their "letters" with the class. We recommend doing the exercise yourself, either the night before or with them, to share what your future script looks like. This provides them with good role modeling; dreams don't end, grown-ups are constantly growing, too.

Next, present the handout Future Scripts, and have students reflect on what they learned about themselves in this exercise, and what they can do with this information. Have them look over their plot and character descriptions for clues about their goals, values, relations with other people, work or career, and lifestyle. Then, have them discuss what might prevent them from realizing this personal vision of their future, and what skills, experiences, contacts, or resources they would need to accomplish it. End the discussion by going around the room and asking each student, "What single step can you take tomorrow to help move you closer to this vision?"

At the conclusion of the exercise, lead into the homework assignment.

4. Assign homework

Ask students to complete the Student Inventory on Life Planning Skills. Also, students should select the lifeskill area for their final project, the growth plan, *before* the next session. In order to participate in Session 11's learning activity, they'll need to identify a short-term and long-term goal for this lifeskill area. Remind them that the selected area can be one of the five lifeskills covered in the course, and another of their own choosing.

FUTURE SCRIPTS

What clues can you find in your character description and plot that indicate values, goals, beliefs? Look at your script for:

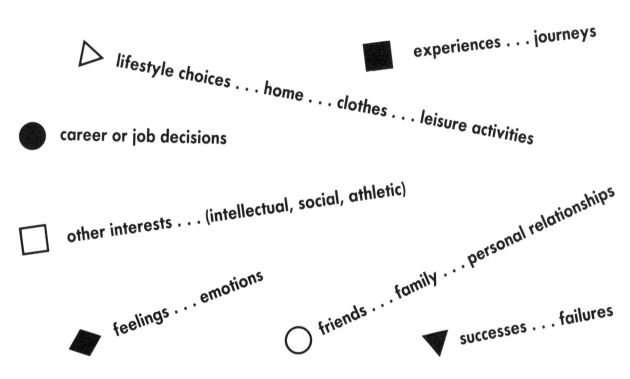

▷ lifestyle choices . . . home . . . clothes . . . leisure activities

■ experiences . . . journeys

● career or job decisions

□ other interests . . . (intellectual, social, athletic)

◆ feelings . . . emotions

○ friends . . . family . . . . personal relationships

▼ successes . . . failures

What is preventing me from pursuing and achieving this vision?

What skills, experiences, contacts, resources do I need?

What single step can I take tomorrow?

STUDENT INVENTORY ON LIFE PLANNING SKILLS

1. Some people live predominantly in the past, some in the present, and others in the future. Right now, you're going to review your past and present in order to reflect on how to plan for the future.

Some people are natural planners. Others resist it. What has been your experience with *planning*? Do you plan your time, your weekly activities, your courses or events for the new season or school year? Why or why not? If you do make efforts to plan these periods, how do you do it?

2. What are the key issues in your life, the big decisions that concern you currently, or have concerned you frequently in the last year? Who influences and/or makes these decisions?

3. Why should you work to identify you interests, values, needs, or goals?

4. How do you currently exercise some control in determining the outcome of these big decisions?

5. When you're 89 years old and looking back on your life, who do you suppose you'll hold responsible for the way your life "turned out?" Why?

Taking control of your life and managing it well takes a long time to develop. Total control of life is not necessarily desirable, even if it were feasible. (A life devoid of spontaneity and unexpected challenges and delights would boring to say the least!) One of the best things a person can learn is expressed in the Serenity Prayer:

> **Grant me the serenity**
> **to accept the things I cannot change,**
> **the courage to change the things I can,**
> **and the wisdom to know the difference.**

Session 11

PLANNING FOR CHANGE

Overview

Planning skills are powerful tools. They can help people change their lives. When people have a sense for where they want to be, planning skills help them get there. If people know who they want to be, planning skills can help them achieve their potential. Even if you're not sure where you're going (and most of us aren't), planning skills are good "exploratory" tools. They can help you seek out information, experiment with change or options in a purposeful way, and structure what may otherwise be a highly stressful period of "not knowing." When people choose to structure their own growth—to plan a desired change—they are taking control of their lives, and asserting themselves as proactive stress managers.

In this session, planning skills are directly applied to the final project. There are three possible topic areas for the growth plan: one of the five lifeskills discussed in the course, a sixth lifeskill area of the student's own choosing, or a life goal identified in Session 10. These plans are developed, in this session, in a cooperative learning group.

Learner Outcomes

The purpose of this session is to enable students to:

1. Apply process steps in preparing a growth plan

2. Brainstorm different steps (e.g., strategies, resources) for their own and other students' growth plans

Agenda

In order to accomplish these outcomes, teachers need to:

1. Supervise small group activity in growth-planning

2. Meet individually with students

3. Collect and assign homework.

Resources and Materials

1. Instructions for Final Project: Growth-Plan (see pages 61-62)

Activities

1. Supervise small group activity

Remind students that taking charge of your life involves creating a personal vision, then planning for changes to bring you closer to that vision. In the growth plan, students have the opportunity to plan for change. This process will be helpful for achieving many goals throughout their lives.

Explain that students will be working in small groups on their final growth plans and meeting with you to ask questions and get support. Divide the class into several small groups and ask them to take out the instruction sheet for this final project (these handouts were first distributed in Session 5, but have extra copies on hand in case they're needed). Groups should be as heterogeneous as possible. For example, males and females should be mixed, minority and majority students should be integrated, and the growth plans should reflect different topic areas. Having a mixture of goals and problems to solve should reduce competition and provide variety to the brainstorm activity.

Explain that the purpose of the group is to help each member to think through the various process steps listed on the instruction sheet. By the end of the session, each student should have at least one suggestion written down for each heading. Students should already have an identified lifeskill area and a short-term and long-term goal. The exercise begins with one student stating his or her area and goals. Then, group members begin to brainstorm. During this session, each student should have a chance to:

■ share with the group his or her selected lifeskill area

- describe his or her long-term and short-term goals within this area

- determine a reasonable goal for the end of the coming term (or year, whatever is appropriate)

- get feedback on (or help determining) what a reasonable measure of success would be, which means defining the degrees of success possible and a set of criteria

- develop several strategies to move closer to this goal

- identify resources (including planned reinforcements) and constraints affecting the outcome

- identify questions he or she needs to answer in order to improve strategies or resources

- translate the plan into a final set of prescriptions, a timetable, or whatever "operationalizes" the strategy (Depending on the strategy, this may not be necessary.)

Remind students about rules for brainstorming: when students offer suggestions (one at a time), the "author" records them without comment. No idea should be criticized, editorialized, or rejected at this point. Members are free to ask the author for information that would help them generate more ideas. When the group seems to have exhausted possibilities for strategies, they should move on to brainstorm resources, reinforcements, and constraints (for the same author, same goal). Again the author takes down the group's suggestions without saying "But . . . but . . . ." After brainstorming, the author may ask for further clarification or problem-solving from the group. She or he will decide, probably after the session is over, which strategies to select and develop.

If the group members are able to work through every one's plan before the session is over, they may use the rest of the period to write their final draft. If students are really listening to each other and thinking through the plans, however, it will probably take the full time period. You can reinforce the group work by circulating the room, sitting in on the discussions, and encouraging students to come up with more ideas. Help them look for ways to challenge, in a supportive way, the goals, criteria, and anticipated problems. The goals is to fortify each plan to its utmost and to encourage each member to strive for a meaningful goal.

This type of cooperative learning may be a new experience for some students, but it can produce fantastic results. When several people put their brains together, the effect on the author—the person requesting their ideas—is empowering. It exercises a student's problem-solving skills several times; the work isn't over when an individual student completes his or her plan. This strategy also reinforces the concept of supportive networks, and provides further reason to believe that students will be supported in making lifeskill changes after the course ends. Several classmates will have invested in the plan!

2. **Meet individually with students**

Students appreciate individual attention with this process. Invite them to schedule an "appointment" to meet with you for five to ten minutes to discuss their concerns with you.

3. **Collect and assign homework**

Collect Student Inventories on Life Planning and have students read pages 103-114 in *Fighting Invisible Tigers* for the final class. Ask if there are any final questions about the audio tape assignment.

Session 12

MOVING ON

Overview

This session is a potpourri of closing activities. It's a time to reflect on the eleven previous sessions and the knowledge gained about stress, coping patterns, and long-term management skills. It's also a time to share future commitments (i.e., growth plan topics and strategies) and to say goodbye. The course is also formally evaluated with a questionnaire. The closing exercise, Affirmations Circle, is used as a send-off.

Learner Outcomes

The purpose of this session is to enable students to:

1. Integrate what they've learned in the course

2. Evaluate the usefulness of course topics, materials, projects, and learning activities

3. Gain group support for their commitments to their growth plans

4. Say goodbye to one another and the teacher

Agenda

In order to accomplish these outcomes, teachers need to:

1. Have students complete the course evaluation questionnaire (10 min.) (See pages 123-125)

2. Lead a group discussion in which students share their growth plan goals and main strategies (15 min.)

3. Hand back the completed sets of student inventories

4. Discuss the final pages in *Fighting Invisible Tigers* (10 min.)

5. Conduct a closing Affirmations Circle (15 min.)

Resources and Materials

1. Course Evaluation Questionnaire (see pages 123-125)

2. Completed student inventories on stress, physical activity, relaxation, assertiveness, relationships, and planning skills

Activities

1. Course evaluation

Students should be given time to complete these questionnaires in class for two reasons: First, the likelihood of getting any back is low if you let students take them home, and second, the process of evaluating a course actually stimulates recall and reinforces what was learned. Filling out the questionnaire, therefore, helps students to integrate course content and goals.

2. Group discussion of final growth plans

In this discussion, students share what they have learned and produced through their final project, the growth plan. Although many of them will already be familiar with some of their peer's plans (through the cooperative learning group in Session 11), they get a chance to present their final plan and learn of others' final solutions in this session. This should help reinforce commitment to them.

Begin by going around the circle and asking students to (briefly) name their long-term and short-term goals, target date, and main strategies. Then ask the student if there are ways in which you or other students in the group can help in future weeks. The idea here is to offer students a chance to ask for help or future reinforcement if they need it. Then proceed around the circle. Don't forget to collect final projects (both the growth plans and audio tapes) at this point. Let them know how and when these projects will be returned.

3. Return inventories

Return the completed student inventories, using the Lifeskills Circle as a cover page (see Session 1) for the six topics covered. (You'll have to spread them on a table and allow students to come find their own number.) Suggest that students reread their inventories after they get home, and evaluate their current level of development in each skill area marked on the circle. If they added another lifeskill to the empty pie slice, evaluate that, too. Tell them to think about "where they were" and what they knew about stress, about relaxation, and all the other lifeskills before the course started. Then, tell them to reflect on what they know now. Rereading their inventories should help them recall the progress they've made. If you wish, also include a copy of the Taxonomy of Lifeskills (see page 10) to help them determine their level of development.

Because the inventories are anonymous you won't be assigning them grades (record them as assignments completed or not). You should, however, respond to students by writing a few comments on each inventory. As with any interactive journal assignment, these comments should be positive, reflective, and more illuminating than judgemental. ("Sounds like this is a very strong feeling you have about sports in this culture." "I'm impressed with your determination to try this strategy." "Do you get this feeling often when you assert yourself?")

When returning the inventories in class, tell students how much you learned from reading them, and how much you appreciate students for sharing them with you. Emphasize that they're beginning a lifelong process of getting to consciously know themselves, and you hope the inventories have stimulated this process. Give them "permission" to periodically examine themselves in journals or discussions with friends.

If there's time, ask students to comment on the final pages in **Fighting Invisible Tigers** concerning perfectionism, humor, and courage. Questions you might ask are:

1. Why is laughter stress-reducing? Why do we need to laugh?

2. What's wrong with perfectionism?

3. How do you know if you're a perfectionist?

4. Why does it take so much courage to use lifeskills?

5. Next time a tiger's got YOU by the tail, what do you think you're going to do: prepare to fight or take flight?

4. Affirmations Circle

This exercise provides closure for the session and the course as well. Have students count off in ones and twos; tell all the ones to form a circle in the middle of the room (standing). Next, tell all the twos to form an outer circle around the ones. (Participate in the outer circle yourself if you have an odd number of students.) Ideally, you should have between seven and eight students in each ring. If you have a very large class (thirty students or more), divide the class into several groups and run the Affirmations Circles simultaneously.

Script for Affirmations Circle

This is called an Affirmations Circle. When I'm through explaining the exercise, I'd like all the students in the outer circle to stand directly behind one of the students in the inner circle, put a hand on his or her shoulder and whisper one positive, encouraging statement in his or her ear. Then stand back. The outer group of students will then rotate to the right to the very next person, and whisper another positive, encouraging remark in his or her ear. Keep these statements sincere, short, and simple; something you would like to hear. I want you to think up your own statements, but just as an example, you might say: "I believe you can do it." "You're not alone." "You've got what it takes." We'll repeat this until the outer circle makes it back to the beginning. Then, the outer and inner groups will change places, and we'll repeat the process.

When the Affirmations Circle is finished, end the class with a rousing standing ovation for all concerned, including you!

Alternative Suggestions

Instead of sharing growth plans, play one or two student's audio relaxation tape(s) and have the whole class do the relaxation exercise. This may be preferable to sharing growth plans if the class is small and a lot of sharing was accomplished in the cooperative learning groups. This does mean that not everyone gets a chance to "show their stuff," but if one student did an especially remarkable job, and you feel the class would enjoy experiencing the tape, this may be a nice way to end the course. If you plan on doing this, you'll need to move the completion deadline for the audio tape up at least one session, so you can screen the projects before this session. You will need to ask the student's permission to play it for the class.

COURSE EVALUATION QUESTIONNAIRE

To help me improve this course, please complete the questions below. All answers will be confidential, so your honesty is sincerely appreciated. To respond, check off ONE box to the right of each question.

Topics

1. How relevant to the subject of stress management were the following topics?

	Irrelevant	Somewhat Relevant	Very Relevant
a) understanding stress	☐	☐	☐
b) physical activity	☐	☐	☐
c) relaxation skills	☐	☐	☐
d) assertiveness skills	☐	☐	☐
e) relationship skills	☐	☐	☐
f) life planning skills	☐	☐	☐

2. How valuable to you, personally, were these topics?

	Not Valuable	Somewhat Valuable	Very Valuable
a) understanding stress	☐	☐	☐
b) physical activity	☐	☐	☐
c) relaxation skills	☐	☐	☐
d) assertiveness skills	☐	☐	☐
e) relationship skills	☐	☐	☐
f) life planning skills	☐	☐	☐

3. Was the amount of time spent on each topic the right amount?

		Not Enough	Just Right	Too Much
a)	understanding stress	☐	☐	☐
b)	physical activity	☐	☐	☐
c)	relaxation skills	☐	☐	☐
d)	assertiveness skills	☐	☐	☐
e)	relationship skills	☐	☐	☐
f)	life planning skills	☐	☐	☐

4. How effective were the various kinds of learning activities?

		Ineffective	Somewhat Effective	Very Effective
a)	teacher presentations	☐	☐	☐
b)	group discussions	☐	☐	☐
c)	progressive relaxation exercises	☐	☐	☐
d)	meditation exercise	☐	☐	☐
e)	aerobic exercise	☐	☐	☐
f)	standing ovation, Moonwalk	☐	☐	☐
g)	assertiveness role-play	☐	☐	☐
h)	communication skill exercise	☐	☐	☐
i)	group brainstorming for growth plan	☐	☐	☐

5. How much did you learn about yourself from the student inventories?

Not A Lot	Some	A Lot
☐	☐	☐

6. How much did you learn about stress management from doing the final projects?

		Not A Lot	Some	A Lot
a)	audio relaxation tape	☐	☐	☐
b)	growth plan	☐	☐	☐

124

7. What was your single favorite feature about this class?

8. What suggestions do you have for improving this course?

Suggestions for topics:

Suggestions for learning activities:

Suggestions for assignments, texts, or other materials:

Suggestions for teacher on teaching style:

Other:

THANK YOU!

PART III

ADDITIONAL TEACHER MATERIALS

LIFESKILLS MATRIX

	Stress Awareness	Physical Activities	Relaxation Skills	Assertiveness Skills	Relationship Skills	Planning Skills
1 Undifferentiated Awareness	Out of touch with self; unaware of physical or emotional effects of stress.	Out of touch with body; little physical activity, unfit, low motivation.	Out of touch with body; unaware of what deep relaxation feels like. Unable to focus, concentrate; fear of quiet.	Cannot distinguish between communication styles. Denies effects of aggression and passivity; unsure of basic rights.	Out of touch with other people; unable to form or sustain close relationships. Denies loneliness, need for others.	Feels controlled by others. Out of touch with own needs, goals, interests. Feels lost, hopeless; lives for moment.
2 Heightened Awareness	Is aware of some stress; can distinguish between physical and emotional stress. Can describe it in others.	Differentiates between different physical activities, between different levels of effort. Reluctant participant; unfit.	Differentiates between high agitation and relaxation; between calm and scattered mind.	Distinguishes between different response styles. Can identify styles in others; verbalizes basic rights but doesn't always respect them in others.	Can differentiate between levels of intimacy; takes few risks; verbalizes need for a range of friends.	Can appreciate the effects of plans; identifies some directions, but lacks confidence and planning skills.
3 Personal Awareness	Describes personal stressors and symptoms; predicts responses given specific triggers.	Can identify some personal strengths and preferences in physical activity. Occasional participant. Begins to plan activity.	Can identify personal benefits from relaxation exercises. Occasionally seeks quiet. Begins to plan for relaxation.	Observes and classifies own response styles; predicts when certain behaviors are likely to emerge. Applies assertiveness consciously in some situations.	Describes communications skills used to gain intimacy; recognizes own role in forming relationships. Reasonably comfortable taking risks, self-disclosure.	Understands personal values, needs, goals to a greater extent. Senses that control over life is possible. Begins to make consistent choices.
4 Proactive Awareness	Avoids negative coping strategies; successfully employs some lifeskills to manage specific stressors.	Makes reasonable choices regarding physical activity. Is starting to become a regular participant; gaining in fitness	Realizes relaxation must be planned; successfully reduces specific stressors with relaxation.	Realizes negative outcomes of passive and aggressive behaviors; accepts responsibility for assertiveness. Is becoming more assertive.	Clarifies needs, thoughts, feelings in relationships; often uses communication skills to form and keep friends.	Overrides group norms and parent's influence when appropriate; negotiates with decision-makers; employs planning and time-management skills often.
5 Internalized Awareness	Incorporates lifeskills with regularity to maintain psychological and physiological health.	Incorporates reasonable physical activities routinely to maintain fitness and reduce stress. Is physically fit.	Incorporates time for relaxation routinely; feels rested, full of energy; enjoys some quiet solitude.	Protects rights for self and respects them in others with assertive communication; asserts self routinely without damaging relationships.	Relates well to a range of people; engenders trust and loyalty by being trustworthy and loyal. Maintains relationships over time.	Periodically clarifies and reaffirms values, goals; makes plans, carries through on decisions; coordinates time well with responsibilities.

GUIDELINES FOR EVALUATING FINAL PROJECTS

How you decide to evaluate these projects and assign students a grade will depend on your particular school and its evaluation system. We recommend using a pass/fail grading system if assessments are required, reserving "fail" only for the student who does not hand in either final project and has been a nonparticipant from the beginning.

Both the relaxation audio tape and growth plans probably have their greatest benefit as teaching tools. Still, they will reveal quite a bit of information to you on things such as:

- how aware students are of their stress levels and patterns or response

- how much students learned about progressive relaxation techniques and concepts

- how much they learned about their own values, needs, goals

- how willing students are to take responsibility for their stress . . . for example, how willing they are to comfort or nurture themselves by purposeful relaxation, and how willing they are to identify and pursue individual goals

- how well students know themselves . . . for example, how well they personalize the relaxation messages on their audio tape; how well they identify potent reinforcements for themselves in their growth plan.

Because our overall aim is to raise students' levels of awareness of stress and use of lifeskills, you'll have to evaluate each student's final project individually in terms of progress made. As a rough measure, we offer the following criteria for evaluating the two final projects:

Relaxation Audio Tape

1. **A personalized script.** Evidence that the student has (for example) selected certain muscle groups to emphasize (indicating that's where his or her stress tends to accumulate), or chooses vocabulary that is personally meaningful. (See the student handout on the relaxation tape for ways to personalize the tape.)

131

2. **Understanding of progressive relaxation concepts.** Uses techniques such as repetition, sequenced suggestions that flow in a logical fashion, calm pace, pauses, positive messages, having a beginning, middle, and end.

3. **Enough care with production (e.g., audible voice, ample time) to make the tape useful to them as a relaxation tool.**

4. **Creativity and unusual care with production of tape** (e.g., good use of music, special poetry added, use of special person to do the reading), for extra bonus points.

For the Growth Plan

1. **Meaningful short-term and long-term goals.** The goals should have genuine meaning for the student. The long-term goal should reflect a personal dream or vision. They sky's the limit on this one ("I'd like to be an ice skating star" is okay). The short-term goal should be ambitious, but more realistic about what can be accomplished by the deadline set forth ("I'd like to get to the rink once a week for the next 10 weeks in order to try out for the advanced class this winter").

2. **A reasonable plan for attaining the short-term goal.** By reasonable, we mean a strategy (or better yet, multiple strategies) that are implementable. (Hiring Stevie Wonder to work with you on your singing is probably not possible.)

3. **A reasonable measure of success has been defined.** ("If I miss two days of skating due to colds, that's okay.")

4. **Evidence that problems have been anticipated and tentative solutions explored.** There's at least one problem with every dream; what is it? How should it be handled so the goal is still obtained?

5. **Evidence that resources, including people, have been identified.**

6. **Personal reinforcements have been defined.** Here's where a student's self-knowledge may be revealed. What works for one student (e.g., a special food or treat) may not work for another who needs a companion, or a schedule, or weekly meetings with a tutor or counselor, etc.

7. **Use of more than one person under resources, and especially thoughtful or creative solutions to problems** (for extra bonus points).

TEACHER'S GUIDE EVALUATION FORM

If you have a moment, please give us some feedback on these course materials. We're particularly interested in hearing from you if you implemented some or all of the sessions in the guide. Thank you.

1. **I implemented the following sessions:**

2. **The class consisted of _____students. (Please relate age, gender, and other characteristics of the students.)**

3. **In general, I would rate the materials in this guide as:**

    ☐ excellent

    ☐ good

    ☐ fair

    ☐ below average

    ☐ poor

4. **The following sections or features were among the material's strongest points:**

5. The following sections or features were among the material's weakest points:

6. I suggest the following changes, additions, or substitutions:

Please send us a summary of the student responses to the Course Evaluation Questionnaire.

What else can you tell us about the success or difficulties you encountered when implementing the course? What suggestions do you have for revision?

If we may use your comments, please sign this form and provide the following information:

Name _____

Signature _____

Address _____

City/State/Zip _____

Phone _____

Return this evaluation form to: **Free Spirit Publishing Inc.**
400 First Avenue North, Suite 616
Minneapolis, MN 55401

BIBLIOGRAPHY

Ardell, D. and Tager, M. *Planning for Wellness: A Guidebook for Achieving Optimal Health*. 3rd ed. Dubuque (Iowa): Kendall/Hunt Publishing Co., 1988.

Burns, D. *Feeling Good: The New Mood Therapy*. New York: New American Library, 1981.

Canfield, J. and Wells, H. *100 Ways to Enhance Self-Concept in the Classroom*. New Jersey: Prentice-Hall, 1976.

Chase, L. *The Other Side of the Report Card: A How-To-Do-It Program for Affective Education*. Illinois: Scott, Foresman and Co., 1975.

Cooper, K. H. *The New Aerobics*. New York: Bantam Books, 1983.

Curtis, J. D. and Detert, R. *How to Relax*. Palo Alto (Cal.): Mayfield Publishing, 1981.

Davis, M., McKay, M. and Eshelman, E. R. *The Relaxation and Stress Reduction Workbook*. 2nd ed. Richmond (Cal.): New Harbinger, 1982.

Phelps, S. and Austin, N. *The Assertive Woman: A New Look*. 2nd rev. ed. San Luis Obispo (Cal.): Impact Publishers, Inc., 1987.

Powell, J. *Why Am I Afraid To Tell You Who I Am?* Valencia (Cal.): Tabor Publishing, 1982.

Raths, L., Merrill, H. and Simon, S. *Values and Teaching*. 2nd ed. Columbus (Ohio): Charles E. Merrill, 1978.

Rubin, T. I. *The Angry Book*. New York: Macmillan Publishing Co., 1970.

Ryan, R. and Travis, J. *Wellness Workbook*. Berkeley (Cal.): Ten Speed Press, 1981.

Schmitz, C. C. and Galbraith, J. *Managing the Social and Emotional Needs of the Gifted*. Minneapolis: Free Spirit Publishing, 1985.

Simon, S., Howe, W. L. and Kirschenbaum, H. *Values Clarification*. New York: Dodd, Mead & Co., Inc., 1985.

Smith, M. J. *When I Say No I Feel Guilty*. New York: Bantam Books, 1985.

Suzuki, S. *Zen Mind Beginners Mind*. New York: Weatherhill, Inc., 1970.

400 First Avenue North
Suite 616
Minneapolis, MN 55401-1730
612/338-2068
FAX 612/337-5050

ORDER TOLL-FREE
1-800-735-7323
Monday thru Friday
8:00 A.M.—5:00 P.M. CST

1 ☐ **PLEASE SEND ME THE FREE SPIRIT CATALOG**

2 NAME AND ADDRESS

NAME _____

ADDRESS _____

CITY/STATE _____ ZIP ☐☐☐☐☐

3 SHIP TO (if different from billing address)

NAME _____

ADDRESS _____

CITY/STATE _____ ZIP ☐☐☐☐☐

4 DAYTIME TELEPHONE _____ (in case we have any questions)

5

TITLE	PRICE	QTY.	TOTAL

6 TOTAL

SHIPPING & HANDLING

For merchandise
totals of:........................Add:
Up to $10.00 ....$3.00
$10.01–$19.99..........$4.00
$20.00–$39.99..........$4.75
$40.00–$59.99..........$6.00
$60.00–$79.99..........$7.50
$80.00–$99.99..........$9.00
$100.00–$149.99....$10.00
$150 or more..............8% of
order total

Orders outside continental
North America **add**
$15.00 to above charges.

7 SUBTOTAL _____

8 SALES TAX (6.5% MN ONLY) **+** _____

9 SHIPPING & HANDLING + _____

10 TOTAL $ _____

TO RECEIVE A FREE COPY OF THE FREE SPIRIT CATALOG, OR TO OBTAIN FREE SPIRIT PUBLICATIONS, PLEASE COMPLETE THIS FORM, ORDER BY TELEPHONE (1-800-735-7323) OR ASK FOR FREE SPIRIT BOOKS AT YOUR LOCAL BOOKSTORE.

METHOD OF PAYMENT

☐ CHECK ☐ P.O. ATTACHED ☐ VISA ☐ MASTERCARD GOOD THROUGH ☐☐ — ☐☐

ACCOUNT # ☐☐☐☐☐☐☐☐☐☐☐☐☐☐☐☐☐

SIGNATURE _____

THANK YOU FOR YOUR ORDER!

SEND TO: Free Spirit Publishing Inc., 400 First Ave. North, Suite 616, Minneapolis MN 55401-1730

OR CALL: 1-800-735-7323
LOCAL: 612-338-2068, **FAX:** 612-337-5050

We offer discounts for quantity purchases.
Write or call for more information.

MORE FREE SPIRIT BOOKS

Making the Most of Today:
Daily Readings for Young People on Self-Awareness, Creativity, and Self-Esteem
by Pamela Espeland and Rosemary Wallner
Guides young people through a year of positive thinking, problem-solving, and practical lifeskills—the keys to making the most of every day.
$8.95; 392 pp; s/c; 4" x 7";
ISBN 0-915793-33-4

The First Honest Book About Lies
by Jonni Kincher
Discusses the nature of lies and helps kids search for truth, become active, intelligent questioners, and explore their own feelings about lies.
$12.95; 200 pp; s/c; illus.; 8" x 10";
ISBN 0-915793-43-1

Kids with Courage: *True Stories about Young People Making a Difference*
by Barbara A. Lewis
Exciting true accounts of kids taking social action, fighting crime, working to save the environment, and performing heroic acts.
$10.95; 160 pp; illus.; s/c; 6" x 9";
ISBN 0-915793-39-3

Talk with Teens about Self and Stress: *50 Guided Discussions for School and Counseling Groups*
by Jean Sunde Peterson
50 guided discussions help students share their feelings and concerns, gain self-awareness and self-esteem, make better decisions, anticipate and solve problems, cope with stress, and more.
$19.95; 192 pp; s/c; 8 1/2"x11"
ISBN 0-915793-55-5

A Teacher's Guide to Fighting Invisible Tigers: *A 12-Part Course in Lifeskills Development*
by Connie Schmitz with Earl Hipp
$16.95; 144 pp; s/c; illus.; 8 1/2" x 11";
ISBN 0-915793-08-3

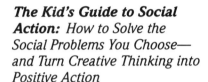

Fighting Invisible Tigers: *A Stress Management Guide for Teens*
by Earl Hipp
For every young person who has ever felt frustrated, overwhelmed, or depressed about life and wants to do something about it.
$9.95; 120 pp; s/c; illus.; 6" x 9";
ISBN 0-915793-04-0

The Kid's Guide to Social Action: *How to Solve the Social Problems You Choose— and Turn Creative Thinking into Positive Action*
by Barbara A. Lewis
A comprehensive guide to making a difference in the world. Teaches letter-writing, interviewing, speech-making, fundraising, lobbying, getting media coverage and more.
$14.95; 208 pp; illus.; B&W photos; s/c;
8 1/2" x 11"; ISBN 0-915793-29-6

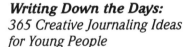

Writing Down the Days: *365 Creative Journaling Ideas for Young People*
by Lorraine M. Dahlstrom
Innovative and fun creative writing assignments for every day of the year. Each entry relates to a person or event that gives special meaning to that day, and each is designed to evoke personal responses an self-discoveries. With topics like these, students will enjoy writing and become better writers.
$12.95; 176 pp; illus; s/c; 6"x9"
ISBN 0-915793-19-9

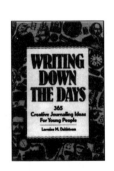

SEE REVERSE FOR ORDER FORM
CALL TOLL-FREE 1(800)735-7323 FOR A FREE CATALOG